PIER PAOLO PASOLINI
POEMS

SELECTED AND TRANSLATED BY

NORMAN MacAFEE

WITH

LUCIANO MARTINENGO

FOREWORD BY

ENZO SICILIANO

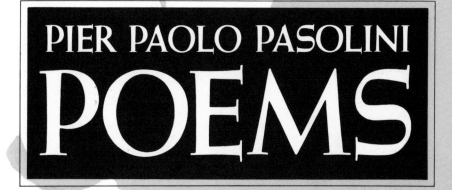

PIER PAOLO PASOLINI

POEMS

VINTAGE BOOKS
A DIVISION OF RANDOM HOUSE
NEW YORK

First Vintage Books Edition, April 1982,

"A Desperate Vitality," translated by Norman MacAfee, first appeared in *Christopher Street*.
"Ashes of Gramsci," translated by Norman MacAfee, first appeared in *The Paris Review*.
"Reality," translated by Norman MacAfee, first appearde in *Unmuzzled Ox*.

Library of Congress Cataloging in Publication Data
Pasolini, Pier Paolo, 1922–1975.
Poems.
Includes bibliographical references.
I. MacAfee, Norman. II. Martinengo, Luciano. III. Title.
PQ4835.A48A25 1982b   851'.914   81-70281
ISBN 0-394-70824-5   AACR2

These translations have received an award from The Translation Center at Columbia University, made possible by a grant from the National Endowment for the Arts.

Manufactured in the United States of America
Typography and binding design by J. K. Lambert
9 8 7 6 5 4 3 2
First Edition

                    The few
friends who came to see me,

new in my new state
of old work, old misery,
on those forgotten mornings

and evenings near the Penitentiary,
saw me bathed in a living light:
a meek, violent revolutionary

in my heart and language. A man was flowering.

—"The Tears of the Excavator"

FOREWORD

BY ENZO SICILIANO

The reader of Pasolini who is unfamiliar with the history of Italian poetry in our century and before should be aware, first of all, of an important tradition in our literature. Italian poetry has had a small number of what are called "civil" poets. When we speak of civil poetry in Italy, we mean poetry in the manner of Victor Hugo, but not only this; we also mean the poetry of the *Divine Comedy*, an example without equal.

In what sense can one speak of Dante's *Divine Comedy* as civil or public poetry? The problem, in my opinion, was put with great simplicity and insight by William Carlos Williams, in his essay of 1939, "Against the Weather: A Study of the Artist." Williams wrote that "the *Divina Commedia* presents three facts, the moral, that of formal religion and that other whose character, in itself, I wish to define. The comment of the artist illuminates the other two—a good place to witness it at work. Dante upon Dante."

Civil poetry, then, is poetry in which abstract subject matter—"moral" and "religious" in Dante's case, and as we know, these can also instantly turn "political"—becomes fused with an entirely personal sensibility, which absorbs every detail, every shading of inspiration into itself and into the transformation of its content into poetic language. It is this sensibility that Williams calls "enlightenment upon the artist's significance" or "Dante upon Dante."

Pasolini is a poet of this kind: his subject matter is "political" and "ideological" and also "religious" (a twentieth-century religiosity, from which all relations with a personalized God are absent). His content, however, does not lie solely within the lines of his poetry, whether they are simply enunciated or transformed into pure decoration, as often occurred in Romantic poetry with a political inspiration: it is involved in an outlook that is the "artist's significance," the import of an artist who in the very act of sharing in certain values, in certain social agitations, questions himself, his role and his destiny, searching in them for the justification for his own writing and his own faith.

The example of Dante is everywhere present in Pasolini. Dante for him is an obligatory point of reference, and not a notably hidden one. We should note that Petrarch, Alfieri, Leopardi and D'Annunzio also wrote poetry that can be called civil; but their poems differ radically from Dante's, and therefore from Pasolini's, in that these four wrote in the name of certain received cultural values of classical humanism that were common to all of European literature. Their defense of the concept of "the homeland," for example, was made in the name of Latin culture, and of the way in which tradition had shaped the inspiring and maternal image of Rome. Dante, even if he was subject to an imperial, Roman dream of his own, speaks in the name of a political party, the Ghibellines, whose defeat and ill fortunes he shared totally, to the point of exile. So with Pasolini, who feels his own inspiration come to life when he joins his voice with that of a social class (broadly speaking, the disinherited and damned of the earth) or when he seeks to answer existential questions with the plan for renewal of the state offered by Marxist socialism.

Having said this, and keeping in mind, too, that we cannot ignore the problem that Williams would have defined as "Pasolini upon Pasolini," one can attempt to draw an interior portrait of the most original poet to appear on the Italian literary scene since Montale.

Pier Paolo Pasolini was born in Bologna on March 5, 1922. A few months later in the same year, fascism would take power in Italy, with Mussolini's march on Rome. The old agrarian, liberal Italy was changing, and in order to resist the shock of the new century and its upheavals, it resorted to a dictatorship that would serve as a model—a sinister model—for several countries of Europe.

It was written in Pasolini's destiny that he would be the poet of various traumatic changes Italy was to undergo in the future: the poet of the transition from a Fascist to a democratic spirit; the poet of the demise of those very democratic ideals, swept aside by the consumer society, by that mass leveling which, in his political journalism written in the early seventies, just before his death, he called "anthropological genocide."

His destiny, however, is marked by more than one paradox, and many questions arise.

What usually strikes us in a writer? That he finds himself struggling against forces which seek to annihilate him: that he strives to manipulate these forces—and they seem to defeat him, and he seems to succumb. That this writer becomes master of the challenge which is issued to him, or that he issues himself: he masters it to the point where he overcomes every resistance. Thus, he destroys every language that has preceded him and creates his own, a new, highly original language.

Very few Italian writers of the rank of Pasolini have provided such visible evidence of a struggle of this sort and of their own victories— at least few in this century. That struggle and those victories, while he was alive, were the occasion for incredulity among many, and for fierce accusations and debate. In this selection from Pasolini's poetry, the reader will find "The Ashes of Gramsci" (1954), a poem new in the history of twentieth-century Italian poetry, for it broke the long chain of "pure" lyric verse, formalistic and of great literary dignity, but deliberately noncommunicative and hermetic in content. Distilling in the traditional Dantesque tercet the daily and intellectual speech of an Italy delivered from fascism, Pasolini in his poem declared himself, as poet and as man, to be the theater of a conflict—between reason and instinct, between moral vocation and inner feeling. That conflict involved not only an individual but a mentality current in the entire country, divided as it was between nostalgia for a dark past and the need for a new liberty, a new justice. Yet most readers, literary critics and others, considered the poem an example of exhibitionism. Such an uproar had not been aroused by the publication of a poem in Italy since the time of D'Annunzio. It was discussed by men of letters as well as by politicians and general readers.

With the death of Pasolini a kind of alchemy has transformed the doubts and refutations that always accompanied his work. Formerly seen as calculating and insincere by many, and dictated only by contingent motives, Pasolini's art was suddenly illuminated by a mythical sincerity. This the redemption of death can accomplish—and especially this particular kind of death, an assassination that occurred on the night between the first and second of November 1975.

But a death of this sort cast an equivocal light on the entire figure of the poet. And because of this we must try not to forget the paradox which that figure irradiates.

Pasolini, about age twenty, wrote poems in Friulian (his mother was from the Friuli region, northeast of Venice) that evoked aspects of ancient troubador poetry; he also wrote poems in Italian, inspired by the sensuality of the great European decadent poetic tradition, which he would collect under the title *L'usignolo della chiesa Cattolica* [*The Nightingale of the Catholic Church*].

How did the delicate poet of *trobar clus*, the passionate reader of Baudelaire, Verlaine and Rimbaud, possessed at the outset of his existential journey by an inspiration that seemed to be ever more strictly contained within the boundaries of pure literature—the poet who considered Machado one of his masters—how did he transform himself into a "civil poet," an "ideological poet," and end his intellectual trajectory in the guise of the political polemicist, the writer of lead articles for the *Corriere della Sera*, a daily newspaper with an extremely wide distribution?

The poet of *Nightingale* or of *La Meglio Gioventù* [*The Finest Youth*], the title of the collection of all his Friulian poems, wrote with the idea in mind that poetry was dead after Rimbaud, and that bringing it back to life must be his practical goal ("O practical end of my poetry," he would write in the early sixties). This poet searched for a similar "practical end" with pertinacity and anguish, day after day, year after year, experiment after experiment, risking the total destruction of his own lyric inspiration and the definitive laceration of his own instinctive sensibility for Italian verse—the hendecasyllable whose rhythm he had been able to revivify yet again as few had done.

In this it is possible to see a parallel with Ezra Pound, though not because there were similarities of subject matter or a relationship between the two poets. (Pasolini failed to understand Pound throughout the sixties: in the end, however, he appreciated his greatness, and wrote and spoke about him with vigorous critical penetration.) If there is a link with Pound, then, it consists in the attempt to join literary, formal choice to a "practical," that is, exhortative, "end"—in order to reach disconsolate frustration. It is useless to point out the opposite directions of Pound's and Pasolini's ends—Pound toward fascistic corporatism, Pasolini toward socialistic and democratic values, which, according to an intensely European line of thought, do not exclude the Marxist and Catholic matrices.

Life and literature: Pasolini bound them tightly together to the point of confusing them, to the point that they canceled each other out, and then, by a miracle, were reborn from their ashes entirely distinct, each with its own appearance, or were sublimated into a utopia similar to a negative theology.

I have said that finally he found his "practical end" in political pam-
phleteering. But the road was a long one: from "The Ashes of Gramsci"
and the novel *Ragazzi di vita* (published in America as *The Ragazzi*), a
picaresque novel dedicated to the life of the Roman slums, from films
like *Accattone* and the *Gospel According to Saint Matthew*, through
the poems of *Trasumanar e organizzar* [To Transfigure, To Organize]
(where all cohesion of the "I" seems to collapse) to the extreme, desolate
image of *Salò*, the posthumous film in which two boys dance a fox trot
together and talk about the sweetheart of one, and so show how it is
possible, with sad innocence, to survive the Nazi slaughter.

Clearly, not a linear journey: and Pasolini certainly lived it the way
one lives life, by daylight, but also with a stunning naturalness.

Among the posthumous works of Pasolini there is a very significant
text in verse entitled "Poeta delle Ceneri," which has recently been
printed in *Nuovi Argomenti* (July–December 1980), the magazine that
Pasolini helped found and edit. It is a long autobiography, pocked with
excisions and revisions, typewritten as if in response to a hypothetical
New York journalist. Pasolini began it in New York in 1966, during
his first trip to the United States. The reader of this book will find the
same themes, almost the same logical organization of material, displayed
in compact form in the essay "To the New Reader" and in the lines of
"Plan of Future Works." But there is one point in the manuscript that
is expressed with shining clarity—a farewell to poetry as such:

> I'd like simply to live
> though being a poet
> because life is expressed only with itself.
> I'd like to express myself by examples.
> To throw my body into the struggle.

The paradox is explained: poetry no longer suffices. "Insofar as I am
a poet I will be a poet of things," writes Pasolini. He embraces action for
the sake of action: his desire for action is such that it propels him to
pronounce decisive, even prophetic words, to make an existential calcula-
tion that adds up to an hallucination: "To throw my body into the
struggle." He who believed as a boy that after Rimbaud poetry was
dead, after having been a poet, celebrates the funeral rite of his own
poetry, sings its dirge.

Politics, "action," were his constant dream—and poetry, in a man who
was literate to the marrow, represented the substitute for that dream.

*   *   *

That he wanted to "act politically" was never a secret. That he was a psychagogue, a prophet, more than a politician, is equally apparent. The root of the thing is doubtless locked in his psychology (in his need to gain a publicly defined role within a society that rejected him because he was homosexual), and in his Neo-Romantic dream of siding, with limitless generosity, with the wretched of the earth, the disinherited of the world, the marginal of every kind. But all of this was also the fruit of his upbringing, an upbringing that happened miraculously to coincide with his psychology, as always occurs in a poet.

From 1942 to 1949, at Casarsa, his mother's birthplace in the Friulian plain, Pasolini had eagerly assimilated a great deal of human and literary experience, which would be transformed into richer and more violent experience in Rome, beginning in 1950 (we are speaking both of his relations with the boys of the urban sub-proletariat and of his reflections on the relations between literature and society).

Feelings of marginality, of moral and physical boundaries, are encouraged in Friuli by geography (to the east lie the mountains of Croatia, to the west the farmland of the Veneto). It was in the first years of adolescence that the poet began to write the dialect poems which he first called *Poems of Casarsa* with the intention of redeeming an obscure mode of speech through brilliance of literary expression. He was convinced that, because of this, the small local communities of very poor Friulian-speaking peasants would become historically self-aware. And he would be the votary of this awareness.

This can seem like the illusion of a young man of letters—and in part it was. It certainly would have been such if nothing else had happened.

It was this philological and linguistic as well as creative experience that led Pasolini to reflect, even then, on "the little homelands," the enduring regional loyalties, of Italy. And this reflection was to stay with him obsessively up to the last moments of his life, in the diatribes written for the *Corriere della Sera* in 1974 and 1975. This theme of the "little homelands" is in itself a political theme. With the end of the Second World War, while the debate on regional separatism was being raised in Italy, Pasolini wrote about a national unity that could only come from the grass roots, taking into consideration all the special and individual linguistic and anthropological characteristics of which the Italian fabric is the sum. In these writings one discovers an intellectual heat that would attain its own moment of greatest power in the idea of "anthropological genocide" which, like an incurable social malady, would become a reality in Italy through political and cultural indifference.

The Friulian Pasolini already had clearly in mind the idea that it is lethal in a collectivity to break, cast aside or forget historical continuity to the point of denying it—and history is a synthesis of languages, customs and usages. The ideal of action, in such a poet, was directed, then, toward the defense of that "continuity," that "historicity."

This being said, it seems clear to me that the adolescent who grew tender and drunk over a stanza of Verlaine, who was so enamored with the medieval lyric of the troubadors in *Poems of Casarsa*, losing himself in the very delicate and inimitable game of rhyme—and his falling in love had been so decisive that it led him to choose the dialect of his mother as his language, since he did not feel the language of official culture was responsive to his own needs—this adolescent nourished within himself, the last flower of the great European decadence, a will to life so consuming that poetic language could only seem inadequate, impoverished, even if sublime in its poverty.

Things, action: what magic was potent in them, and what rapacious truth. "To throw my body into the struggle": this is the true dream of existence for the poet Pasolini, or the knot that binds everything together.

He felt he was not "understood": he experienced, in the blazing controversy that always accompanied his intellectual "action," the profound frustration of one who regularly encounters misunderstanding—and one must say that, with his taste for self-contradiction, he certainly loved to play with the fire of incomprehension. And to overcome all this—without realizing that he was falling into a vortex of self-destruction—he resolved as the crowning work of his life to do what everything he wrote summarized: "Throw my body into the struggle." Not a book, but an act.

Death is not
in not being able to communicate
but in no longer being able to be understood.

The reader of this book will find these lines in "A Desperate Vitality." There he will see every formal concern of the poet dissolved, his inspiration burned to ashes in an anxiety that is quasi-gestural and no longer expressive.

The desire for action—"the practical end" of poetry—is for Pasolini what the flight into Abyssinia was for Rimbaud.

Once the illusions of the economic boom in Italy had faded with the end of the sixties, and a gloomy, cruel period that is still not over had begun, the significance of "throwing himself into the struggle" became more complex for Pasolini. He tried to write polemical journalism as in his years in Friuli; he wrote for weeklies, involving himself in exchanges of correspondence with readers. But this kind of expression did not seem enough for him. He wrote:

The actions of life alone will be communicated
and these will be poetry.

Writing for a daily like the *Corriere della Sera* seemed to realize this thirst for "communication."

He had said to Jean-Michel Gardair, in an interview published in *Le Monde* on February 26, 1971, "I can no longer believe in revolution, but I cannot fail to be on the side of the young who are fighting for it. It's already an illusion to write poetry, and yet I continue doing so, even if for me poetry is no longer the marvelous classical myth that exalted my adolescence. I no longer believe in dialectic and contradiction, but only in opposition. Still, I am ever more fascinated by the exemplary alliance which is achieved in the saints, like Saint Paul, between the active life and the contemplative life."

Psychagogue, prophet, he no longer believed that the instruments of reason and literature could reconcile the past with the present, or life with poetry. Active and contemplative at once, he wrote his "Letters to the Romans" for the mass media.

He struggled against "bourgeois entropy," against the uniform acceptance of customs he considered "heinous," and once again took the risk of being misunderstood, misconstrued, refuted. And so it happened.

The ultimate meaning of his "struggle," notwithstanding the obscure significance of his death at the seaplane basin at Ostia, lies in a spasmodic and never-satisfied will to live.

—*translated from the Italian
by Jonathan Galassi*

CONTENTS

PART FOUR

THE ASHES OF GRAMSCI

GRAMSCI

(1957)

PART ONE

I

Non è di maggio questa impura aria
che il buio giardino straniero
fa ancora più buio, o l'abbaglia

con cieche schiarite . . . questo cielo
di bave sopra gli attici giallini
che in semicerchi immensi fanno velo

alle curve del Tevere, ai turchini
monti del Lazio. . . . Spande una mortale
pace, disamorata come i nostri destini,

tra le vecchie muraglie l'autunnale
maggio. In esso c'è il grigiore del mondo
la fine del decennio in cui ci appare

tra le macerie finito il profondo
e ingenuo sforzo di rifare la vita;
il silenzio, fradicio e infecondo. . . .

Tu giovane, in quel maggio in cui l'errore
era ancora vita, in quel maggio italiano
che alla vita aggiungeva almeno ardore,

quanto meno sventato e impuramente sano
dei nostri padri—non padre, ma umile
fratello—già con la tua magra mano

delineavi l'ideale che illumina
(ma non per noi: tu, morto, e noi
morti ugualmente, con te, nell'umido

giardino) questo silenzio. Non puoi,
lo vedi?, che riposare in questo sito
estraneo, ancora confinato. Noia

I

It isn't May-like, this impure air
which darkens the foreigners' dark
garden still more, then dazzles it

with blinding sunlight . . . this foam-
streaked sky above the ocher roof
terraces which in vast semicircles veil

Tiber's curves and Latium's cobalt
mountains. . . . Inside the ancient walls
the autumnal May diffuses a deathly

peace, disquieting like our destinies,
and holds the whole world's dismay,
the finish of the decade that saw

the profound naïve struggle to make
life over collapse in ruins;
silence, humid, fruitless . . .

Young man, in that May when to err meant
one was still alive, in that Italian May
which at least gave life fire, you,

so much less thoughtless and impurely sane
than our fathers—but not father: rather, humble
brother—even then with your thin hand, you

were sketching the ideal that illuminates
(but not for us: you, dead, and we
dead too with you in this humid garden)

this silence. You must know you can't do
any more than rest, confined even now
in this extraneous earth. Patrician ennui

patrizia ti è intorno. E, sbiadito,
solo ti giunge qualche colpo d'incudine
dalle officine di Testaccio, sopito

nel vespro: tra misere tettoie, nudi
mucchi di latta, ferrivecchi, dove
cantando vizioso un garzone già chiude

la sua giornata, mentre intorno spiove.

II

Tra i due mondi, la tregua, in cui non siamo.
Scelte, dedizioni . . . altro suono non hanno
ormai che questo del giardino gramo

e nobile, in cui caparbio l'inganno
che attutiva la vita resta nella morte.
Nei cerchi dei sarcofaghi non fanno

che mostrare la superstite sorte
di gente laica le laiche iscrizioni
in queste grige pietre, corte

e imponenti. Ancora di passioni
sfrenate senza scandalo son arse
le ossa dei miliardari di nazioni

più grandi; ronzano, quasi mai scomparse,
le ironie dei principi, dei pederasti,
i cui corpi sono nell'urne sparse

inceneriti e non ancora casti.
Qui il silenzio della morte è fede
di un civile silenzio di uomini rimasti

uomini, di un tedio che nel tedio
del Parco, discreto muta: e la città
che, indifferente, lo confina in mezzo

surrounds you. And the only sound that reaches you
is the faded hammer blow on an anvil
from the workshops of Testaccio, drowsy

in the evening, with its shacks of poverty, its
naked piles of tin cans and scrap iron, where
singing, leering, an apprentice already is

ending his day, while the last raindrops fall.

II

Between the two worlds, the truce in which
we don't exist. Choices, allegiances . . .
By now their only sound is this bleak

noble garden's, where the deceit that
diminished life stubbornly persists in death.
In the circles of the sarcophagi,

on these grey, low, stately stones,
secular epitaphs announce only
the surviving fates of secular

people. The bones of millionaires
from mightier nations are still burning
with unrestrained passions, without scandal.

Never completely vanishing, the ironies
of princes and pederasts ceaselessly
buzzing, their bodies in their scattered urns,

though merely ashes now, remain impure.
The silence of death testifies here
to a civil silence of men who still are

men, to a tedium, which, in the Park's
tedium, discreetly changes; and
the uncaring city, banishing him

a tuguri e a chiese, empia nella pietà,
vi perde il suo splendore. La sua terra
grassa di ortiche e di legumi dà

questi magri cipressi, questa nera
umidità che chiazza i muri intorno
a smorti ghirigori di bosso, che la sera

rasserenando spegne in disadorni
sentori d'alga . . . quest'erbetta stenta
e inodora, dove violetta si sprofonda

l'atmosfera, con un brivido di menta,
o fieno marcio, e quieta vi prelude
con diurna malinconia, la spenta

trepidazione della notte. Rude
di clima, dolcissimo di storia, è
tra questi muri il suolo in cui trasuda

altro suolo; questo umido che
ricorda altro umido; e risuonano
— familiari da latitudini e

orizzonti dove le selve inglesi coronano
laghi spersi nel cielo, tra praterie
verdi come fosforici biliardi o come

smeraldi: « And O ye Fountains . . . »—le pie
invocazioni. . . .

III

Uno straccetto rosso, come quello
arrotolato al collo ai partigiani
e, presso l'urna, sul terreno cereo,

diversamente rossi, due gerani.
Lì tu stai, bandito e con dura eleganza
non cattolica, elencato tra estranei

amid slums and churches, here,
impious in its piety, loses its splendor.
Its earth, rich with nettles and clover,

nourishes these thin cypresses, this black
humidity that stains the walls behind
pale contorted boxwood, which the reassuring

evening extinguishes into unembellished
inklings of seaweed . . . this sparse, scentless
grass, into which, with a shiver

of mint or rotten hay, the violet
twilight sinks, quietly foreshadowing
with daylight melancholy the night's

exhausted trepidations. Harsh
the climate, sweet the history of the earth
within these walls, earth mixing with

other earth; this moisture
recalling other moisture; and—familiar
from latitudes and horizons

where English glades crown lakes lost
in the heavens, amid meadows green as
phosphorescent billiard tables or

emeralds: "And O ye Fountains . . ."—resound the pious
invocations . . .

III

A scrap of red cloth, like those the Partisans
knotted up around their necks
and, near the urn, on the waxen earth,

a different red, of two geraniums.
There you lie, banished, listed with severe
non-Catholic elegance, among the foreign

morti: Le ceneri di Gramsci . . . Tra speranza
e vecchia sfiducia, ti accosto, capitato
per caso in questa magra serra, innanzi

alla tua tomba, al tuo spirito restato
quaggiù tra questi liberi. (O è qualcosa
di diverso, forse, di più estasiato

e anche di più umile, ebbra simbiosi
d'adolescente di sesso con morte . . .)
E, da questo paese in cui non ebbe posa

la tua tensione, sento quale torto
—qui nella quiete delle tombe—e insieme
quale ragione—nell'inquieta sorte

nostra—tu avessi stilando le supreme
pagine nei giorni del tuo assassinio.
Ecco qui ad attestare il seme

non ancora disperso dell'antico dominio,
questi morti attaccati a un possesso
che affonda nei secoli il suo abominio

e la sua grandezza: e insieme, ossesso,
quel vibrare d'incudini, in sordina,
soffocato e accorante—dal dimesso

rione—ad attestarne la fine.
Ed ecco qui me stesso . . . povero, vestito
dei panni che i poveri adocchiano in vetrine

dal rozzo splendore, e che ha sbiadito
la sporcizia delle più sperdute strade,
delle panche dei tram, da cui stranito

è il mio giorno: mentre sempre più rade
ho di queste vacanze, nel tormento
del mantenermi in vita; e se mi accade

dead: The ashes of Gramsci . . . Between hope
and my old distrust, I approach you,
chancing upon this thinned-out greenhouse, before

your tomb, before your spirit, still alive
down here among the free. (Or it's
something else, perhaps more ecstatic, even

humbler: an intoxicated, adolescent
symbiosis of sex and death . . .)
And in this land where your passion never

rested, I feel how wrong
—here, among the quiet of these graves—
and yet how right—in our unquiet

fate—you were, as you drafted your final
pages in the days of your murder.
Here, attesting to the still-not-dispersed seeds

of their ancient domination, lie these
dead men possessed by a greed
that buries its grandeur and abomination

deep in the centuries; and at the same time,
attesting to its end: obsessed
striking of anvils, stifled, softly

grieving, coming from the humble quarter.
And here am I . . . poor, dressed in
clothes that the poor admire in store

windows for their crude splendors
and that filthy back streets and tram
benches (which daze my day)

have faded; while, less and less often, these
moments come to me to interrupt my torment
of staying alive; and if I happen

di amare il mondo non è che per violento
e ingenuo amore sensuale
così come, confuso adolescente, un tempo

l'odiai, se in esso mi feriva il male
borghese di me borghese: e ora, scisso
—con te—il mondo, oggetto non appare

di rancore e quasi di mistico
disprezzo, la parte che ne ha il potere?
Eppure senza il tuo rigore, sussisto

perché non scelgo. Vivo nel non volere
del tramontato dopoguerra: amando
il mondo che odio—nella sua miseria

sprezzante e perso—per un oscuro scandalo
della coscienza . . .

IV

Lo scandalo del contraddirmi, dell'essere
con te e contro te; con te nel cuore,
in luce, contro te nelle buie viscere;

del mio paterno stato traditore
—nel pensiero, in un'ombra di azione—
mi so ad esso attaccato nel calore

degli istinti, dell'estetica passione;
attratto da una vita proletaria
a te anteriore, è per me religione

la sua allegria, non la millenaria
sua lotta: la sua natura, non la sua
coscienza; è la forza originaria

dell'uomo, che nell'atto s'è perduta,
a darle l'ebbrezza della nostalgia
e una luce poetica: ed altro più

to love the world, it's a naïve
violent sensual love, just as I
hated it when I was a confused

adolescent and its bourgeois evils
wounded my bourgeois self; and now, divided—
with you—doesn't the world—or at least

that part which holds power—seem worthy only
of rancor and an almost mystical contempt?
Yet without your rigor, I survive because

I do not choose. I live in the non-will
of the dead postwar years: loving
the world I hate, scorning it, lost

in its wretchedness—in an obscure scandal
of consciousness . . .

IV

The scandal of contradicting myself, of being
with you and against you; with you in my heart,
in light, but against you in the dark viscera;

traitor to my paternal state
—in my thoughts, in the shadows of action—
I know I'm attached to it, in the heat

of the instincts and aesthetic passion;
attracted to a proletarian life
that preceded you; for me it is a religion,

its joy, not its millennial
struggle; its nature, not its
consciousness. Only the originating force

of man, which he lost in becoming man,
could give it this intoxicating
nostalgia, this poetic light—and more

io non so dirne, che non sia
giusto ma non sincero, astratto
amore, non accorante simpatia ...

Come i poveri povero, mi attacco
come loro a umilianti speranze,
come loro per vivere mi batto

ogni giorno. Ma nella desolante
mia condizione di diseredato,
io possiedo: ed è il più esaltante

dei possessi borghesi, lo stato
più assoluto. Ma come io possiedo la storia,
essa mi possiede; ne sono illuminato:

ma a che serve la luce?

    v

Non dico l'individuo, il fenomeno
dell'ardore sensuale e sentimentale ...
altri vizi esso ha, altro è il nome

e la fatalità del suo peccare ...
Ma in esso impastati quali comuni,
prenatali vizi, e quale

oggettivo peccato! Non sono immuni
gli interni e esterni atti, che lo fanno
incarnato alla vita, da nessuna

delle religioni che nella vita stanno,
ipoteca di morte, istituite
a ingannare la luce, a dar luce all'inganno.

Destinate a esser seppellite
le sue spoglie al Verano, è cattolica
la sua lotta con esse: gesuitiche

I don't know how to say than what is
just but not sincere, abstract
love, not grieving fellow-feeling . . .

Poor as the poor I cling,
like them, to humiliating hopes;
like them, each day I nearly kill myself

just to live. But though
desolated, disinherited
I possess (and it's the most exalting

bourgeois possession of all) the most
absolute condition. But while I possess history,
it possesses me. I'm illuminated by it;

but what's the use of such light?

v

I'm not speaking of the individual, that
phenomenon of sensual and sentimental passions . . .
he has other vices; nor will I speak

of the name of his sin or its fatal destiny . . .
But oh the common prenatal vices
and the indisputable sins enmeshed

deep inside him! The actions, internal,
external, that incarnate him in life
are not immune to those

religions that, in life, mortgage
death, established to deceive
the light and shed light on the deceit.

His remains are destined to be
buried in the Verano; his struggle
with them is Catholic: the manias with

le manìe con cui dispone il cuore;
e ancor più dentro: ha bibliche astuzie
la sua coscienza . . . e ironico ardore

liberale . . . e rozza luce, tra i disgusti
di dandy provinciale, di provinciale
salute . . . Fino alle infime minuzie

in cui sfumano, nel fondo animale,
Autorità e Anarchia . . . Ben protetto
dall'impura virtù e dall'ebbro peccare,

difendendo una ingenuità di ossesso,
e con quale coscienza!, vive l'io: io,
vivo, eludendo la vita, con nel petto

il senso di una vita che sia oblio
accorante, violento . . . Ah come
capisco, muto nel fradicio brusio

del vento, qui dov'è muta Roma,
tra i cipressi stancamente sconvolti,
presso te, l'anima il cui graffito suona

Shelley . . . Come capisco il vortice
dei sentimenti, il capriccio (greco
nel cuore del patrizio, nordico

villeggiante) che lo inghiottì nel cieco
celeste del Tirreno; la carnale
gioia dell'avventura, estetica

e puerile: mentre prostrata l'Italia
come dentro il ventre di un'enorme
cicala, spalanca bianchi litorali,

sparsi nel Lazio di velate torme
di pini, barocchi, di giallognole
radure di ruchetta, dove dorme

which he prepares his heart are Jesuitical;
and still deeper inside: his conscience has
Biblical cunning . . . and ironic liberal

passion . . . and crass brightness, amid
the aversions of a provincial dandy, of
provincial normality . . . Down to the minutest trifles,

where Authority and Anarchy vanish
into animal depths . . . Secure
against impure virtue and intoxicated sin,

defending an obsessive ingenuousness—
and with what conscience!—thus lives the I: I
alive, eluding life, while the feeling grows

of a life becoming grieving
violent oblivion . . . Ah, how well
I understand, silent in the wind's wet

humming, here where Rome is silent,
among wearily agitated cypresses,
next to you, Spirit whose inscription calls out

Shelley . . . How well I understand the vortex
of feelings, the capricious fate (Grecian
in the aristocratic Northern traveler's

heart) which swallowed him in the dazzling
turquoise Tyrrhenian Sea; the carnal
joy of adventure, aesthetic

and boyish—while prostrate Italy,
as though inside the belly of an enormous
cicada, bursts open with white coastlines

in Latium brushed here and there with veiled
swarms of baroque pines and delicate
yellow glades of heather, where a young

col membro gonfio tra gli stracci un sogno
goethiano, il giovincello ciociaro . . .
Nella Maremma, scuri, di stupende fogne

d'erbasaetta in cui si stampa chiaro
il nocciòlo, pei viottoli che il buttero
della sua gioventù ricolma ignaro.

Ciecamente fragranti nelle asciutte
curve della Versilia, che sul mare
aggrovigliato, cieco, i tersi stucchi,

le tarsie lievi della sua pasquale
campagna interamente umana,
espone, incupita sul Cinquale,

dipanata sotto le torride Apuane,
i blu vitrei sul rosa . . . Di scogli,
frane, sconvolti, come per un panico

di fragranza, nella Riviera, molle,
erta, dove il sole lotta con la brezza
a dar suprema soavità agli olii

del mare . . . E intorno ronza di lietezza
lo sterminato strumento a percussione
del sesso e della luce: così avvezza

ne è l'Italia che non ne trema, come
morta nella sua vita: gridano caldi
da centinaia di porti il nome

del compagno i giovinetti madidi
nel bruno della faccia, tra la gente
rivierasca, presso orti di cardi,

in luride spiaggette . . .

Mi chiederai tu, morto disadorno,
d'abbandonare questa disperata
passione di essere nel mondo?

Roman peasant dozes, penis swollen
among his rags, a Goethean dream . . . Coastlines
in Maremma darkened by stupendous pools

of adders' tongue, in which the hazel bush
is sharply etched, along footpaths the shepherd
unknowingly fills to the brim with his youth.

Blindly fragrant coastlines in Versilia
whose drying curves expose to the blind
entangled sea the terse stuccoes

and light patchworks of its Eastertide
completely human countryside,
darkened on the Cinquale, unraveling

at the foot of the torrid Apuan
Alps, glasslike blues on pink . . .
Landsliding coastlines convulsed as though by

a panic of fragrance on the steep, languid
Riviera, where sun struggles with breeze
to confer supreme suavity upon the sea's

oils . . . And everywhere the boundless
percussion instrument of sex and light
buzzes joyfully: so used is Italy to it

she doesn't even tremble, as though
dead in her life; fervently,
young men with tan sweaty faces

shout the name of their comrade, from
hundreds of ports, among the Riviera's
people, in backyard cardoon gardens,

on small filthy beaches . . .

Will you ask me, unadorned dead man,
to abandon this desperate
passion to be in the world?

Me ne vado, ti lascio nella sera
che, benché triste, così dolce scende
per noi viventi, con la luce cerea

che al quartiere in penombra si rapprende.
E lo sommuove. Lo fa più grande, vuoto,
intorno, e, più lontano, lo riaccende

di una vita smaniosa che del roco
rotolìo dei tram, dei gridi umani,
dialettali, fa un concerto fioco

e assoluto. E senti come in quei lontani
esseri che, in vita, gridano, ridono,
in quei loro veicoli, in quei grami

caseggiati dove si consuma l'infido
ed espansivo dono dell'esistenza—
quella vita non è che un brivido;

corporea, collettiva presenza;
senti il mancare di ogni religione
vera; non vita, ma sopravvivenza

—forse più lieta della vita—come
d'un popolo di animali, nel cui arcano
orgasmo non ci sia altra passione

che per l'operare quotidiano:
umile fervore cui dà un senso di festa
l'umile corruzione. Quanto più è vano

—in questo vuoto della storia, in questa
ronzante pausa in cui la vita tace—
ogni ideale, meglio è manifesta

la stupenda, adusta sensualità
quasi alessandrina, che tutto minia
e impuramente accende, quando qua

VI

I'm leaving, leaving you in the evening
which though sad descends so sweetly
for us the living, as its waxen light

curdles in the twilit neighborhood.
And stirs it, makes it everywhere larger,
emptier, and, in the distance, rekindles it

with yearning life, which, using harsh
rumbling trams and human shouts
in dialect, performs a faintly heard, absolute

concert. And you feel—like those distant
beings, who in life shout and laugh
in those vehicles of theirs, in those bleak

tenements where the untrustworthy expansive
gift of existence is consumed—
that life is only a shiver:

corporeal collective presence:
you feel the lack of any true
religion: not life but survival

—maybe happier than life—as with
a people of animals in whose arcane
orgasmic excitement there is no other

passion than for daily work: humble
fervor that gives a festive air to
humble corruption. The emptier each

ideal—in this vacuum of history,
in this buzzing pause when life is
silent—the more obvious the awesome,

ancient, almost Alexandrian
sensuality, which impurely decorates
all with golden light when there

nel mondo, qualcosa crolla, e si trascina
il mondo, nella penombra, rientrando
in vuote piazze, in scorate officine . . .

Già si accendono i lumi, costellando
Via Zabaglia, Via Franklin, l'intero
Testaccio, disadorno tra il suo grande

lurido monte, i lungoteveri, il nero
fondale, oltre il fiume, che Monteverde
ammassa o sfuma invisibile sul cielo.

Diademi di lumi che si perdono,
smaglianti, e freddi di tristezza
quasi marina . . . Manca poco alla cena;

brillano i rari autobus del quartiere,
con grappoli d'operai agli sportelli,
e gruppi di militari vanno, senza fretta,

verso il monte che cela in mezzo a sterri
fradici e mucchi secchi d'immondizia
nell'ombra, rintanate zoccollette

che aspettano irose sopra la sporcizia
afrodisiaca: e, non lontano, tra casette
abusive ai margini del monte, o in mezzo

a palazzi, quasi a mondi, dei ragazzi
leggeri come stracci giocano alla brezza
non più fredda, primaverile; ardenti

di sventatezza giovanile la romanesca
loro sera di maggio scuri adolescenti
fischiano pei marciapiedi, nella festa

vespertina; e scrosciano le saracinesche
dei garages di schianto, gioiosamente,
se il buio ha resa serena la sera,

in the world something collapses and the world
drags itself along, in the twilight, reentering
the empty piazzas, the disheartened workshops . . .

The streetlamps have awakened, studding
Via Zabaglia, Via Franklin, the entire
Testaccio, naked with its lurid

hill, the streets along the Tiber, and across
the river, the black backdrop that Monteverde
amasses then disperses invisibly into the sky . . .

Diadems of light losing themselves,
dazzling, cold, with almost
sea-like sadness . . . It's nearly suppertime;

the quarter's few buses shine with clusters
of workers clinging to their doors, while
bunches of soldiers stroll, not hurrying,

toward the hill, which conceals amid rotten
excavations and dry mounds of garbage
the shadowy nests of whores waiting

angrily atop that aphrodisiac
filth; and not far off, near illegal shacks
next to the Mount or surrounded

by buildings that are nearly worlds, boys
light as rags play in the breeze,
no longer cold, of springtime; burning with

juvenile thoughtlessness, dark adolescents
whistle their native Roman night of May
along the sidewalks of the evening

feast; and garages' rolling shutters
roar down joyously when the dark
has made the evening serene, and among

e in mezzo ai platani di Piazza Testaccio
il vento che cade in tremiti di bufera,
è ben dolce, benché radendo i capellacci

e i tufi del Macello, vi si imbeva
di sangue marcio, e per ogni dove
agiti rifiuti e odore di miseria.

È un brusio la vita, e questi persi
in essa, la perdono serenamente,
se il cuore ne hanno pieno: a godersi

eccoli, miseri, la sera: e potente
in essi, inermi, per essi, il mito
rinasce . . . Ma io, con il cuore cosciente

di chi soltanto nella storia ha vita,
potrò mai più con pura passione operare,
se so che la nostra storia è finita?

(1954)

the plane trees in Piazza Testaccio,
the wind, dying with shivers of storms,
is good and sweet, though grazing the coarse hairs

and tufa of the slaughterhouses, it gets
soaked in rotten blood and everywhere
agitates the refuse and odor of poverty.

It is a dim hum, life, and those lost
in it serenely lose it, if their
hearts are filled with it. Here they are,

the wretched enjoying the evening. And potent
in them, the defenseless, through them, the myth
is reborn . . . But I with the conscious heart

of one who can live only in history,
will I ever again be able to act with pure passion
when I know our history is over?

(1954)

IL PIANTO DELLA SCAVATRICE

I

Solo l'amare, solo il conoscere
conta, non l'aver amato,
non l'aver conosciuto. Dà angoscia

il vivere di un consumato
amore. L'anima non cresce più.
Ecco nel calore incantato

della notte che piena quaggiù
tra le curve del fiume e le sopite
visioni della città sparsa di luci,

echeggia ancora di mille vite,
disamore, mistero, e miseria
dei sensi, mi rendono nemiche

le forme del mondo, che fino a ieri
erano la mia ragione d'esistere.
Annoiato, stanco, rincaso, per neri

piazzali di mercati, tristi
strade intorno al porto fluviale,
tra le baracche e i magazzini misti

agli ultimi prati. Lì mortale
è il silenzio: ma giù, a viale Marconi,
alla stazione di Trastevere, appare

ancora dolce la sera. Ai loro rioni,
alle loro borgate, tornano su motori
leggeri—in tuta o coi calzoni

di lavoro, ma spinti da un festivo ardore—
i giovani, coi compagni sui sellini,
ridenti, sporchi. Gli ultimi avventori

THE TEARS OF THE EXCAVATOR

Only loving, only knowing
matter, not past love
nor past knowledge. Living

a consummated love
is agonizing. The soul no longer grows.
And in the dark enchanted heat,

down here along the curving
river with its drowsy sights
of the city touched with lights,

the night still echoes with a thousand lives;
while the estrangement, mystery, misery
of the senses cut me off from

the world's shapes, which were till
yesterday my reason for living.
Bored, tired, I return home, across

dark marketplaces, down sad streets
near the river docks between shacks
and warehouses mingling with the countryside's

last fields, where there's a deathly
silence, though farther along, at Viale Marconi,
at Trastevere Station, the evening's

still sweet. To their neighborhoods,
their slums, the young return on light
motorbikes, in overalls and workpants;

but propelled by festive fire,
with a friend behind on the saddle
laughing and dirty. In the night

chiacchierano in piedi con voci
alte nella notte, qua e là, ai tavolini
dei locali ancora lucenti e semivuoti.

Stupenda e misera città,
che m'hai insegnato ciò che allegri e feroci
gli uomini imparano bambini,

le piccole cose in cui la grandezza
della vita in pace si scopre, come
andare duri e pronti nella ressa

delle strade, rivolgersi a un altro uomo
senza tremare, non vergognarsi
di guardare il denaro contato

con pigre dita dal fattorino
che suda contro le facciate in corsa
in un colore eterno d'estate;

a difendermi, a offendere, ad avere
il mondo davanti agli occhi e non
soltanto in cuore, a capire

che pochi conoscono le passioni
in cui io sono vissuto:
che non mi sono fraterni, eppure sono

fratelli proprio nell'avere
passioni di uomini
che allegri, inconsci, interi

vivono di esperienze
ignote a me. Stupenda e misera
città che mi hai fatto fare

esperienza di quella vita
ignota: fino a farmi scoprire
ciò che, in ognuno, era il mondo.

the last customers stand talking
loudly, amid the little tables of nearly
empty but still brightly lit cafés.

Stupendous, miserable city,
you taught me what men learn
joyously and ferociously as children,

those little things in which we
discover life's grandeur in peace:
going tough and ready into crowded

streets, addressing another man
without trembling, not ashamed
to check the change counted

by the lazy fingers of the conductor
sweating along passing façades
in the eternal red of summer;

to defend myself, to attack, to have
the world before my eyes and not
just in my heart, to understand

that few know the passions
in which I've lived; that they're
not brotherly to me, and yet they are

my brothers because they have
passions of men
who, joyous, unknowing, whole,

live experiences
unknown to me. Stupendous, miserable
city, you made me

experience that unknown
life, you made me discover
what the world was for everyone.

Una luna morente nel silenzio,
che di lei vive, sbianca tra violenti
ardori, che miseramente sulla terra

muta di vita, coi bei viali, le vecchie
viuzze, senza dar luce abbagliano
e, in tutto il mondo, le riflette

lassù, un po' di calda nuvolaglia.
È la notte più bella dell'estate.
Trastevere, in un odore di paglia

di vecchie stalle, di svuotate
osterie, non dorme ancora.
Gli angoli bui, le pareti placide

risuonano d'incantati rumori.
Uomini e ragazzi se ne tornano a casa
—sotto festoni di luci ormai sole—

verso i loro vicoli, che intasano
buio e immondizia, con quel passo blando
da cui più l'anima era invasa

quando veramente amavo, quando
veramente volevo capire.
E, come allora, scompaiono cantando.

II

Povero come un gatto del Colosseo,
vivevo in una borgata tutta calce
e polverone, lontano dalla città

e dalla campagna, stretto ogni giorno
in un autobus rantolante:
e ogni andata, ogni ritorno

era un calvario di sudore e di ansie.
Lunghe camminate in una calda caligine,
lunghi crepuscoli davanti alle carte

A moon dying in the silence that she
feeds goes white amid violent glowing,
which, miserably, on the silent earth,

with its beautiful avenues and old
lanes, dazzles them without shedding
light, while a few hot cloud masses

reflect them to her, above, all over the world.
It's the most beautiful night of summer.
Trastevere, which smells of emptied

taverns and straw from old
stables, isn't asleep yet.
Its dark corners and peaceful walls

resound with enchanted sounds.
Men and boys are strolling home
—beneath abandoned garlands of lights—

toward their alleyways clogged by
darkness and garbage, with that slow pace
which invaded the depths of my soul

when I truly loved, when
I truly wanted to understand.
And, as then, they disappear, singing.

II

Poor as a cat in the Coliseum,
I lived in a slum of dust clouds
and limestone, far from city,

far from countryside, squeezed each day
onto a wheezing bus;
and every trip back and forth

was a calvary of sweat and anxiety—
long walks in the heat's haze,
long dusks in front of my papers

ammucchiate sul tavolo, tra strade di fango,
muriccioli, casette bagnate di calce
e senza infissi, con tende per porte . . .

Passavano l'olivaio, lo straccivendolo,
venendo da qualche altra borgata,
con l'impolverata merce che pareva

frutto di furto, e una faccia crudele
di giovani invecchiati tra i vizi
di chi ha una madre dura e affamata.

Rinnovato dal mondo nuovo,
libero—una vampa, un fiato
che non so dire, alla realtà

che umile e sporca, confusa e immensa,
brulicava nella meridionale periferia,
dava un senso di serena pietà.

Un'anima in me, che non era solo mia,
una piccola anima in quel mondo sconfinato,
cresceva, nutrita dall'allegria

di chi amava, anche se non riamato.
E tutto si illuminava, a questo amore
forse ancora di ragazzo, eroicamente,

e però maturato dall'esperienza
che nasceva ai piedi della storia.
Ero al centro del mondo, in quel mondo

di borgate tristi, beduine,
di gialle praterie sfregate
da un vento sempre senza pace,

venisse dal caldo mare di Fiumicino,
o dall'agro, dove si perdeva
la città fra i tuguri; in quel mondo

heaped on the table, among muddy streets,
low walls, small whitewashed
windowless shacks that had curtains for doors . . .

The olive vendor, the ragman passed by,
coming from some other slum, with their
dusty merchandise that looked like

stolen goods . . . with their cruel faces of young
men aging amid the vices of those
whose mothers have grown hard in hunger.

Renewed by the new world,
free—a fiery flare, an indescribable
breath gave a sense of serene

piety to that humble,
sordid, confused, immense reality
swarming in those southern slums.

A soul within me, not just mine,
a little soul in that boundless world,
was growing, fed by the joy

of one who loves, though his love is unrequited.
And everything filled with light because of this love.
It was perhaps still a young boy's heroic love,

and yet matured by experience
born at the foot of history.
I was in the center of the world, in that

world of sad Bedouin slum towns
and yellow prairies chafed
by a relentless wind

from the warm sea of Fiumicino
or the countryside, where the city
disintegrated among hovels, in that world

che poteva soltanto dominare,
quadrato spettro giallognolo
nella giallognola foschia,

bucato da mille file uguali
di finestre sbarrate, il Penitenziario
tra vecchi campi e sopiti casali.

Le cartacce e la polvere che cieco
il venticello trascinava qua e là,
le povere voci senza eco

di donnette venute dai monti
Sabini, dall'Adriatico, e qua
accampate, ormai con torme

di deperiti e duri ragazzini
stridenti nelle canottiere a pezzi,
nei grigi, bruciati calzoncini,

i soli africani, le piogge agitate
che rendevano torrenti di fango
le strade, gli autobus ai capolinea

affondati nel loro angolo
tra un'ultima striscia d'erba bianca
e qualche acido, ardente immondezzaio ...

era il centro del mondo, com'era
al centro della storia il mio amore
per esso: e in questa

maturità che per essere nascente
era ancora amore, tutto era
per divenire chiaro—era,

chiaro! Quel borgo nudo al vento,
non romano, non meridionale,
non operaio, era la vita

which could be dominated only by
the penitentiary, square ocher
specter in the ocher haze,

pierced by a thousand identical
rows of barred windows, amid
ancient fields and drowsy farmhouses.

Dust and trash blindly
lofted by the light wind,
the poor echoless voices

of humble women, emigrants from the Sabine
hills or the Adriatic,
camping here with swarms of tough

malnourished shrieking kids
in ragged undershirts
and faded grey shorts

in the African sunlight and the agitated rains
that made streets muddy torrents,
buses mired at the end

of the line, at a corner formed by
a last bleached grass-streak
and some fermenting garbage heap . . .

this was the center of the world,
as my love for it was at
the center of history: and in this

maturity only then beginning, there was
love nonetheless; everything was
about to become clear—in fact, everything

was clear! Those slums, naked
in the wind, not Roman, not Southern,
not working class, were life

nella sua luce più attuale:
vita, e luce della vita, piena
del caos non ancora proletario,

come la vuole il rozzo giornale
della cellula, l'ultimo
sventolio del rotocalco: osso

dell'esistenza quotidiana,
pura, per essere fin troppo
prossima, assoluta per essere

fin troppo miseramente umana.

III

E ora rincaso, ricco di quegli anni
così nuovi che non avrei mai pensato
di saperli vecchi in un'anima

a essi lontana, come a ogni passato.
Salgo i viali del Gianicolo, fermo
da un bivio liberty, a un largo alberato,

a un troncone di mura—ormai al termine
della città sull'ondulata pianura
che si apre sul mare. E mi rigermina

nell'anima—inerte e scura
come la notte abbandonata al profumo—
una semenza ormai troppo matura

per dare ancora frutto, nel cumulo
di una vita tornata stanca e acerba . . .
Ecco Villa Pamphili, e nel lume

che tranquillo riverbera
sui nuovi muri, la via dove abito.
Presso la mia casa, su un'erba

in its most pertinent light:
life, light of life, full
of a chaos not yet proletarian

(as the local Cell's rough newspaper
and the latest waving of the weekly
magazine claim it is): bone

of daily existence,
pure because so
near, absolute because

all too miserably human.

III

And now I walk home, rich with those years
that were so fresh I never thought I'd see
them old, in my (to them) distant soul—the way

it is with any past. I climb the tree-lined
avenues of the motionless Janiculum,
from an Art-Nouveau crossroads to a shady

square or stretch of wall—by now I'm
at the city limits, overlooking the undulating
plain that opens to the sea. And a seed

already too ripe to bear fruit
germinates once more in my soul—
inert and murky as the night

abandoned to its perfumes—in the pile-up
of a life again grown weary and bitter . . .
Here's Villa Pamphili, and in the light

quietly reflected on new
walls, the street where I live.
Near my house, on grass

ridotta a un'oscura bava,
una traccia sulle voragini scavate
di fresco, nel tufo—caduta ogni rabbia

di distruzione—rampa contro radi palazzi
e pezzi di cielo, inanimata,
una scavatrice . . .

Che pena m'invade, davanti a questi attrezzi
supini, sparsi qua e là nel fango,
davanti a questo canovaccio rosso

che pende a un cavalletto, nell'angolo
dove la notte sembra più triste?
Perché, a questa spenta tinta di sangue,

la mia coscienza così ciecamente resiste,
si nasconde, quasi per un ossesso
rimorso che tutta, nel fondo, la contrista?

Perché dentro in me è lo stesso senso
di giornate per sempre inadempite
che è nel morto firmamento

in cui sbianca questa scavatrice?

Mi spoglio in una della mille stanze
dove a via Fonteiana si dorme.
Su tutto puoi scavare, tempo: speranze

passioni. Ma non su queste forme
pure della vita . . . Si riduce
ad esse l'uomo, quando colme

siano esperienza e fiducia
nel mondo . . . Ah, giorni di Rebibbia,
che io credevo persi in una luce

di necessità, e che ora so così liberi!

reduced to a dark streak,
a trail on chasms freshly dug
in the clay, all destructive

rage spent—a lifeless ramp
against sparse buildings and patches of sky:
an excavator . . .

Why does such grief invade me, facing
these tools scattered in the mud,
in front of this red warning flag

hanging from a sawhorse in that corner
where the night seems saddest?
Why, facing this faded shade of blood,

does my conscience so blindly resist
and hide, as if obsessed by
a remorse that deeply saddens it?

Why is there within me the same sense
of days forever unfulfilled
that fills the dead firmament, under which

this excavator rests, turned white by night?

I undress in one of Via Fonteiana's
thousand rooms where people sleep.
You can quarry into anything, time: hopes,

passions, but not these pure shapes
of life . . . which man is
reduced to, when experience

and trust in the world
are achieved . . . Ah, days at Rebibbia
which I thought lost in a light

of need and which I know now were so free!

Insieme al cuore, allora, pei difficili
casi che ne avevano sperduto
il corso verso un destino umano,

guadagnando in ardore la chiarezza
negata, e in ingenuità
il negato equilibrio—alla chiarezza

all'equilibrio giungeva anche,
in quei giorni, la mente. E il cieco
rimpianto, segno di ogni mia

lotta col mondo, respingevano, ecco,
adulte benché inesperte ideologie . . .
Si faceva, il mondo, soggetto

non più di mistero ma di storia.
Si moltiplicava per mille la gioia
del conoscerlo—come

ogni uomo, umilmente, conosce.
Marx o Gobetti, Gramsci o Croce,
furono vivi nelle vive esperienze.

Mutò la materia di un decennio d'oscura
vocazione, se mi spesi a far chiaro ciò
che più pareva essere ideale figura

a una ideale generazione;
in ogni pagina, in ogni riga
che scrivevo, nell'esilio di Rebibbia,

c'era quel fervore, quella presunzione,
quella gratitudine. Nuovo
nella mia nuova condizione

di vecchio lavoro e di vecchia miseria,
i pochi amici che venivano
da me, nelle mattine o nelle sere

Along with my heart, then, among
the hardships and hazards that had diverted
its progress toward a human fate,

my mind—gaining in passion the denied
clarity, and in ingenuousness
the denied equilibrium—

was in those days finally attaining
clarity and equilibrium. And blind
regret, mark of my whole struggle with

the world, was being rejected by ideologies
that were mature though not experienced. . . .
The world was becoming the subject

no longer of mystery but of history.
The joy of knowing it—as
everyone, humbly, knows it—

grew a thousandfold.
Marx or Gobetti, Gramsci or Croce,
were alive in the life of my experience.

The subject matter of a decade's obscure
vocation changed, when I gave all I had
to clarify what seemed the ideal image

for an ideal generation;
on every page, in every line I
wrote during the Rebibbia exile,

there was that passion, assumption,
gratitude. The few
friends who came to see me,

new in my new state
of old work, old misery,
on those forgotten mornings

dimenticate sul Penitenziario,
mi videro dentro una luce viva:
mite, violento rivoluzionario

nel cuore e nella lingua. Un uomo fioriva.

IV

Mi stringe contro il suo vecchio vello,
che profuma di bosco, e mi posa
il muso con le sue zanne di verro

o errante orso dal fiato di rosa,
sulla bocca: e intorno a me la stanza
è una radura, la coltre corrosa

dagli ultimi sudori giovanili, danza
come un velame di pollini ... E infatti
cammino per una strada che avanza

tra i primi prati primaverili, sfatti
in una luce di paradiso ...
Trasportato dall'onda dei passi,

questa che lascio alle spalle, lieve e misero,
non è la periferia di Roma: « *Viva
Mexico!* » è scritto a calce o inciso

sui ruderi dei templi sui muretti ai bivii,
decrepiti, leggeri come osso, ai confini
di un bruciante cielo senza un brivido.

Ecco, in cima a una collina
fra le ondulazioni, miste alle nubi,
di una vecchia catena appenninica,

la città, mezza vuota, benché sia l'ora
della mattina, quando vanno le donne
alla spesa—o del vespro che indora

and evenings near the Penitentiary,
saw me bathed in a living light:
a meek, violent revolutionary

in my heart and language. A man was flowering.

   IV

He's holding me against his old
sylvan fleece and, with his boar's
or wandering bear's fangs, lays his

muzzle on my mouth, breathing a rose's
breath; and all around me the room's
a clearing, and the blanket, corroded

by the last sweat of youth, dances
like swarms of pollen . . . And in fact
I walk along a road advancing

into spring's first meadows
dissolving in a light of paradise . . .
Carried along on the wave of my steps,

light-hearted, poor, I leave behind me,
not Rome's remote slums: "Viva
Mexico!" is dabbed with whitewash and scratched

in temple ruins, on low walls at crossroads
decayed and light like bones, at the edges
of a sky on fire, unshivering.

Here on top of a hill among
undulations mixing with the clouds
of an old Apennine range

is the city, half empty, though
it's the time of morning when women go out
shopping—or of evening, which lights up

i bambini che corrono con le mamme
fuori dai cortili della scuola.
Da un gran silenzio le strade sono invase:

si perdono i selciati un po' sconnessi,
vecchi come il tempo, grigi come il tempo,
e due lunghi listoni di pietra

corrono lungo le strade, lucidi e spenti.
Qualcuno, in quel silenzio, si muove:
qualche vecchia, qualche ragazzetto

perduto nei suoi giuochi, dove
i portali di un dolce Cinquecento
s'aprano sereni, o un pozzetto

con bestioline intarsiate sui bordi
posi sopra la povera erba,
in qualche bivio o canto dimenticato.

Si apre sulla cima del colle l'erma
piazza del comune, e fra casa
e casa, oltre un muretto, e il verde

d'un grande castagno, si vede
lo spazio della valle: ma non la valle.
Uno spazio che tremola celeste

o appena cereo . . . Ma il Corso continua,
oltre quella famigliare piazzetta
sospesa nel cielo appenninico:

s'interna fra case più strette, scende
un po' a mezza costa: e più in basso
—quando le barocche casette diradano—

ecco apparire la valle—e il deserto.
Ancora solo qualche passo
verso la svolta, dove la strada

golden children running with their
mothers from the school's courtyards.
Vast silence invades the streets:

the loosed cobblestone pavements
are lost, as old and grey
as time; and two long stripes of stone,

smooth and lifeless, line the roads.
Someone moves in that silence,
some old woman, some boy

lost in his games, as the gates
of a sweet sixteenth century open
serenely and a fountain edged with

reliefs of graceful little animals
watches over patchy grass at some
forgotten crossroads or corner.

On the hilltop, the lonely municipal
square comes into view; between houses,
past a wall and the foliage

of a large chestnut tree, one can see
the hollow of the valley, but not the valley itself.
A shivering space, pale blue

or barely waxen . . . But the main street goes on
beyond that familiar little piazza
suspended in the Apennine sky,

continues among denser houses, descends
a bit halfway downhill; and farther below,
when the little baroque houses thin out,

there appears the valley—and the desert.
Then, a few more steps
toward the bend where the road

è già tra nudi praticelli erti
e ricciuti. A manca, contro il pendio,
quasi fosse crollata la chiesa,

si alza gremita di affreschi, azzurri,
rossi, un'abside, pèsta di volute
lungo le cancellate cicatrici

del crollo—da cui soltanto essa,
l'immensa conchiglia, sia rimasta
a spalancarsi contro il cielo.

È lì, da oltre la valle, dal deserto,
che prende a soffiare un'aria, lieve, disperata,
che incendia la pelle di dolcezza . . .

È come quegli odori che, dai campi
bagnati di fresco, o dalle rive di un fiume,
soffiano sulla città nei primi

giorni di bel tempo: e tu
non li riconosci, ma impazzito
quasi di rimpianto, cerchi di capire

se siano di un fuoco acceso sulla brina,
oppure di uve o nespole perdute
in qualche granaio intiepidito

dal sole della stupenda mattina.
Io grido di gioia, così ferito
in fondo ai polmoni da quell'aria

che come un tepore o una luce
respiro guardando la vallata

. . . .

turns through steep curly
naked gardens. At the left, leaning against
the slope as if the church had crumbled,

dense with blue and red frescoes,
an apse, erect, dark with stone
scrolls along the erased scars

of the collapse—out of which
only the immense shell remains,
gaping against the sky.

There, from beyond the valley and the desert,
a light desperate breeze begins to blow,
sweetly inflaming the skin . . .

It's like those smells from freshly
bathed fields or the river's shores
blowing toward the city in the first

days of good weather; and you
can't quite place them and, almost
crazy with regret, try to discover

if they come from fire lit on frost
or grapes or medlars lost
in some granary warmed by this

stupendous morning's sun.
I shout with joy, wounded
to the depths of my lungs by this air

I breathe like light or warmth
as I contemplate the valley

. . . .

v

Un po' di pace basta a rivelare
dentro il cuore l'angoscia,
limpida, come il fondo del mare

in un giorno di sole. Ne riconosci,
senza provarlo, il male
lì, nel tuo letto, petto, coscie

e piedi abbandonati, quale
un crocifisso—o quale Noè
ubriaco, che sogna, ingenuamente ignaro

dell'allegria dei figli, che
su lui, i forti, i puri, si divertono . . .
Il giorno è ormai su di te,

nella stanza come un leone dormente.

Per quali strade il cuore
si trova pieno, perfetto anche in questa
mescolanza di beatitudine e dolore?

Un po' di pace . . . E in te ridesta
è la guerra, è Dio. Si distendono
appena le passioni, si chiude la fresca

ferita appena, che già tu spendi
l'anima, che pareva tutta spesa,
in azioni di sogno che non rendono

niente . . . Ecco, se acceso
alla speranza—che, vecchio leone
puzzolente di vodka, dall'offesa

sua Russia giura Krusciov al mondo—
ecco che tu ti accorgi che sogni.
Sembra bruciare nel felice agosto

v

A bit of peace is enough to reveal
inside the heart an anxiety
clear as the floor of the sea on a day

bright with sunlight. You recognize,
without feeling it, its pain,
there, in your bed, your chest, thighs,

feet abandoned, like someone
crucified—or like Noah
drunk, dreaming, naïvely oblivious

of his derisive sons, so strong,
so pure, laughing over him . . .
Now the daylight's all over you,

in the room, like a sleeping lion.

By which roads does the heart come to
its full perfection, even in this
mix of pain and bliss?

A bit of peace . . . And in you reawake
the war, and God. The passions
are only slightly pacified, the fresh wound's

barely healed, when you spend
the soul, which seemed already fully spent
in dream actions ending in

nothing . . . Now the old
lion, stirred by hope,
reeking of vodka, from his offended

Russia, Khrushchev swears to the world—
now you realize you are dreaming.
All your passions, all your interior

di pace, ogni tua passione, ogni
tuo interiore tormento,
ogni tua ingenua vergogna

di non essere—nel sentimento—
al punto in cui il mondo si rinnova.
Anzi, quel nuovo soffio di vento

ti ricaccia indietro, dove
ogni vento cade: e lì, tumore
che si ricrea, ritrovi

il vecchio crogiolo d'amore,
il senso, lo spavento, la gioia.
E proprio in quel sopore

è la luce . . . in quella incoscienza
d'infante, d'animale o ingenuo libertino
è la purezza . . . i più eroici

furori in quella fuga, il più divino
sentimento in quel basso atto umano
consumato nel sonno mattutino.

VI

Nella vampa abbandonata
del sole mattutino—che riarde,
ormai, radendo i cantieri, sugli infissi

riscaldati—disperate
vibrazioni raschiano il silenzio
che perdutamente sa di vecchio latte,

di piazzette vuote, d'innocenza.
Già almeno dalle sette, quel vibrare
cresce col sole. Povera presenza

d'una dozzina d'anziani operai,
con gli stracci e le canottiere arsi
dal sudore, le cui voci rare,

torment, all your naïve
shame at not living—
in your feelings—at that point

where the world renews itself,
seem to burn in the happy August of peace.
Yet that new breath of wind

pushes you back to where all
winds subside; and there, you, tumor
that renews itself, you find once more

the old crucible of love,
the senses, terror, joy.
And there in that drowsiness is the light . . .

in that innocence that a baby
or animal or ingenuous libertine has
is true purity . . . the most heroic fury is

in that escape, the most godly
feeling in that base human act
consummated in morning sleep.

VI

In the abandoned flame of the morning's
burning sun, already brushing
the construction sites, warming

the wood frames—desperate
vibrations scrape the silence,
which ineffably smells of old milk,

of empty little piazzas and innocence.
Since at least seven o'clock, that vibration
has grown, with the sun. Poor presence

of a dozen old workers,
their rags and undershirts scorched
by sweat, whose infrequently sounding voices

le cui lotte contro gli sparsi
blocchi di fango, le colate di terra,
sembrano in quel tremito disfarsi.

Ma tra gli scoppi testardi della
benna, che cieca smembra, cieca
sgretola, cieca afferra,

quasi non avesse meta,
un urlo improvviso, umano,
nasce, e a tratti si ripete,

così pazzo di dolore, che, umano,
subito non sembra più, e ridiventa
morto stridore. Poi, piano,

rinasce, nella luce violenta,
tra i palazzi accecati, nuovo, uguale,
urlo che solo chi è morente,

nell'ultimo istante, può gettare
in questo sole che crudele ancora splende
già addolcito da un po' d'aria di mare . . .

A gridare è, straziata
de mesi e anni di mattutini
sudori—accompagnata

dal muto stuolo dei suoi scalpellini,
la vecchia scavatrice: ma, insieme, il fresco
sterro sconvolto, o, nel breve confine

dell'orizzonte novecentesco,
tutto il quartiere . . . È la città,
sprofondata in un chiarore di festa,

—è il mondo. Piange ciò che ha
fine e ricomincia. Ciò che era
area erbosa, aperto spiazze, e si fa

and struggles against the scattered
blocks of mud and sliding earth
seem to dissolve in that trembling.

But amid the stubborn explosions of the
rock-crusher, which blindly dismembers, blindly
crumbles, blindly grabs,

as though without direction,
a sudden human scream is born
and periodically returns,

so crazed with pain it seems suddenly
human no longer and becomes once more
a dead screech. Then slowly it's

reborn in the violent light
among the blinded buildings, a new
steady scream that only someone dying,

in his last moment, could hurl
into this sun, which still cruelly shines,
though softened by touches of sea air . . .

The scream is the old excavator's,
tortured by months and years
of morning sweat—accompanied

by silent swarms of stone-
cutters; but it's also the freshly
convulsed earth's, or, within the narrower

limits of the modern horizon,
the whole neighborhood's . . . It is the city's,
plunged into a festive brilliance

—it is the world's. The crying is for
what ends and begins again—what was
grass and open space and has become

cortile, bianco come cera,
chiuso in un decoro ch'è rancore;
ciò che era quasi una vecchia fiera

di freschi intonachi sghembi al sole,
e si fa nuovo isolato, brulicante
in un ordine ch'è spento dolore.

Piange ciò che muta, anche
per farsi migliore. La luce
del futuro non cessa un solo istante

di ferirci: è qui, che brucia
in ogni nostro atto quotidiano,
angoscia anche nella fiducia

che ci dà vita, nell'impeto gobettiano
verso questi operai, che muti innalzano,
nel rione dell'altro fronte umano,

il loro rosso straccio di speranza.

(1956)

waxy white courtyards
enclosed within a resentful decorum;
what was almost an old fairground

of bright plaster slanting in the sun
and has become a new block, swarming
in an order made of stifled grief.

The crying is for what changes, even if
to become something better. The light
of the future doesn't cease for even an instant

to wound us: it is here to
brand us in all our daily deeds
with anxiety even in the confidence

that gives us life, in the Gobettian impulse
toward these workers, who silently raise, in this
neighborhood of the other human vanguard,

their red rag of hope.

(1956)

THE RELIGION OF MY TIME

(1961)

PART TWO

Due giornate di febbre! Tanto

da non poter più sopportare l'esterno,
se appena un po' rinnovato dalle nubi
calde, di ottobre, e così moderno

ormai—che mi pare di non poterlo più
capire—in quei due che salgono la strada
là in fondo, all'alba della gioventù ...

Disadorni, ignorati: eppure fradici
sono i loro capelli d'una beata crosta
di brillantina—rubata nell'armadio

dei fratelli maggiori; oppure losca
di millenari soli cittadini
la tela dei calzoni al sole d'Ostia

e al vento scoloriti; eppure fini
i lavori incalliti del pettine
sul ciuffo a strisce bionde e sulla scrima.

Dall'angolo d'un palazzo, eretti,
appaiono, ma stanchi per la salita,
e scompaiono, per ultimi i garretti,

all'angolo d'un altro palazzo. La vita
è come se non fosse mai stata.
Il sole, il colore del cielo, la nemica

dolcezza, che l'aria rabbuiata
da redivive nubi, ridà alle cose,
tutto accade come a una passata

ora del mio esistere: misteriose
mattine di Bologna o di Casarsa,
doloranti e perfette come rose,

Two days of fever! Too much, so I

can't endure the outside world anymore,
even though it's somewhat refreshed by
October's hot clouds, and so modern now

I feel I'll never again understand it,
in those two climbing the street
down there, at the dawn of youth.

Unadorned, unknown, and yet their hair
gleams with a joyful layer
of brilliantine, stolen from older

brothers' closets; and their
wind-faded trousers are bleached
by thousand-year-old city suns

in Ostia's sunshine; and fine
are their combs' labors stiffened
on the part and the forelock's blond streaks.

At the corner of a building, they appear,
erect though tired from climbing,
then disappear, ankles the last,

at the corner of another building.
Now it seems like life had never been.
Sun, sky's color, the hostile

sweetness which the air, darkened
by reviving clouds, returns to everything:
All of this is happening as though

in an earlier hour of my life;
mysterious mornings of Bologna,
Casarsa, aching, perfect as roses,

riaccadono qui nella luce apparsa
a due avviliti occhi di ragazzo,
che altro non conosce se non l'arte

di perdersi, chiaro nel suo buio arazzo.
E non ho mai peccato: sono
puro come un vecchio santo, ma

neppure ho avuto; il dono
disperato del sesso, è andato
tutto in fumo: sono buono

come un pazzo. Il passato
è quello che ebbi per destino,
niente altro che vuoto sconsolato . . .

e consolante. Osservo, chino
sul davanzale, quei due nel sole
andare, lievi; e sto come un bambino

che non geme per ciò che non ha avuto solo,
ma anche per ciò che non avrà . . .
E in quel pianto il mondo è odore,

nient'altro: viole, prati, che sa
mia madre, e in quali primavere . . .
Odore che trema per diventare, qua

dove il pianto è dolce, materia
d'espressione, tono . . . la ben nota
voce della lingua folle e vera

ch'ebbi nascendo e nella vita è immota.

                    *

L'ossessione è perduta, è divenuta
odorante fantasma che si stende
in giorni di luce grande e muta,

here recur in light flashing
in the humiliated eyes of a boy
who knows only the art of losing himself,

luminous in his shadowy tapestry.
And I've never sinned;
I'm pure like some old saint, but that's

gained me nothing; the desperate
gift of sex has gone
up into smoke: I'm good

like a madman. Destiny
gave me the past, but it's only
an emptiness . . . disconsolate . . .

consoling. Leaning on the window sill,
I observe those two lightly moving
in the sun; and I feel like a boy

who moans for what he hasn't had
as well as what he'll never have . . .
And in that weeping, the world is solely

odor: violets and meadows
my mother knows, and in those springtimes . . .
odor trembling, here where tears

are sweet, to become material
for expression, nuance . . . the familiar
voice of that mad true language

I had at birth and in life is still.

    *

The obsession's vanished, become
aromatic phantasm fanning out
in days of great and silent light

quando così debole si accende
l'azzurro che bianco è quasi,
ai rumori dispersi si rapprende

l'assurdo silenzio di stasi
naturali, e agli odori dei pranzi,
dei lavori, si mischiano randagi

soffi di bosco, sepolti nei canti
più ombrosi o più assolati
delle prime colline—stanchi

moti quasi di altre età, ora beati
in questa, che vuole nuovo amore.
Da bambino sognavo a questi fiati,

già freschi e intiepiditi dal sole,
frammenti di foreste, celtiche
quercie, tra sterpaglia e rovi di more

sfrondati, nel rossore, quasi svèlti
dall'autunno assolato—e seni
di fiumi nordici ciecamente deserti,

dove pungeva l'odore dei licheni,
fresco e nudo, come di Pasqua le viole . . .
Allora la carne era senza freni.

E la dolcezza ch'era nel colore
del giorno, si faceva dolcezza
un poco anche in quel dolore.

La gioventù bendata, rozza, retta
delle famiglie barbare che andavano
emigrando, per la sommessa

selva o l'allagata plaga
consolavano la solitudine
del mio lettuccio, della mia strada.

when blue sky ignites
so pale it's almost white
and gathers scattered noises

into the absurd silence of nature's pauses;
and smells of meals and work
mix with wandering breezes

from woods buried in sunny
or shadowy shelters of foothills,
weary movements seemingly

come from other ages, but joyful
in our time, which wants new love.
As a boy, I'd dream of these

fresh sun-warmed breezes,
forest fragments, Celtic oaks,
shrubs and leafless blackberry

bushes, red, ripening, nearly uprooted
by the sunlit autumn—and the inlets
of blindly deserted Northern rivers

with their sharp smell of lichen,
cool and naked like Easter's violets . . .
Flesh was unchained then.

And the sweetness that was
in the day's color very nearly
sweetened even that pain.

Ragged young men, rough, erect,
from barbarian families migrating
endlessly through hushed forests

and along the flooded plains
consoled the solitude
of my narrow bed, my road.

La storia, la Chiesa, la vicissitudine
d'una famiglia, così, non sono
che un po' di sole profumato e nudo,

che riscalda una vigna in abbandono,
qualche filo di fieno tra i boschetti
corrosi, qualche casa tramortita al suono

delle campane . . . I giovinetti
antichi, essi soltanto vivi, se pieni
della primavera ebbero i petti

nelle età più belle, erano insieme
sogni del sesso e immagini bevute
dalla vecchia carta del poema

che di volume in volume, in mute
febbri di novità suprema,
—erano Shakespeare, Tommaseo, Carducci . . .—

faceva d'ogni mia fibra un solo tremito.

                    *

Avrei voluto urlare, e ero muto;
la mia religione era un profumo.
Ed eccolo ora qui, uguale e sconosciuto,

quel profumo, nel mondo, umido
e raggiante: e io qui, perso nell'atto
sempre riuscito e inutile, umile

e squisito, di scioglierne l'intatto
senso nelle sue mille immagini . . .
Mi ritrovo tenero come un ragazzo

all'entusiasmo misterioso, selvaggio,
come fu in passato, e stente
lacrime mi bagnano la pagina

History, the Church, a family's
vicissitudes, are really
just some naked perfumed sun

warming a deserted vineyard, some rows
of hay in corroded groves,
a few houses stunned by the sound

of bells . . . Young men of ancient times,
truly living when their breasts
filled up with spring in those more

beautiful ages, were simultaneously
dreams of sex and images drunk up
out of the old paper of the poem

which from volume to volume, in mute
fevers of supreme newness
—Shakespeare, Tommaseo, Carducci—

made all my nerves one tremor.

    *

I wanted to shout but went mute;
my religion was a perfume.
And now, humid, radiant,

it has returned to the world, still that same
unknown perfume; and here am I, lost in the act,
always successful and useless, humble

and exquisite, of liberating intact
meaning from its thousand images . . .
I become once again tender as a boy

with his savage mysterious eagerness,
as in the past, and difficult
tears wet my page at the sight

alla vista, nel solicello ardente,
di quei due, che—loro sì ragazzi—
si perdono svelti, beatamente,

nella ricca periferia, sotto terrazzi
pieni di sereno cielo di mare,
mattutini balconi, attici

dorati da un sole già serale . . .
Il senso della vita mi ritorna
com'era sempre allora, un male

più cieco se stupendamente colmo
di dolcezza. Perché, a un ragazzo, pare
che mai avrà ciò che egli solo

non ha mai avuto. E in quel mare
di disperazione, il suo furioso sogno
di corpi, crede di dover pagare

con l'essere follemente buono . . .

Così, se bastano due giorni
di febbre, perché la vita sembri
perduta e intero torni

il mondo (e niente m'inebbri
altro che rimpianto) al mondo io,
nel grande e muto sole di settembre,

morendo, non saprei che dire addio . . .

Eppure, Chiesa, ero venuto a te.
Pascal e i Canti del Popolo Greco
tenevo stretti in mano, ardente, come se

il mistero contadino, quieto
e sordo nell'estate del quarantatre,
tra il borgo, le viti e il greto

in the sweetly burning sunlight
of those two boys, still so young,
quickly joyfully getting lost

in wealthy suburbs, below terraces
full of serene sea sky or the balconies
of morning or rooftops painted

gold by an already twilit sun . . .
The sense comes back to me of life
as it always was then, an affliction

even blinder because wondrously filled
with sweetness. For a boy always feels
he'll never have what he alone

has never had. And in that desperate
sea, his furious dream
of bodies, he believes he has to pay

by being insanely good . . .

So, if two days of fever
suffice for life to seem
lost and that world to return

intact (and nothing but regret
to intoxicate me), dying, in September's
giant silent sun, I wouldn't know

what to say to the world but good-by . . .

And yet, Church, I came to you.
I was holding Pascal and *The Songs
of the Greek People* tightly in my hand,

ardent, as though the peasant mystery,
quiet and deaf in the summer of '43,
among the village, vines, and banks

del Tagliamento, fosse al centro
della terra e del cielo;
e lì, gola, cuore e ventre

squarciati sul lontano sentiero
delle Fonde, consumavo le ore
del più bel tempo umano, l'intero

mio giorno di gioventù, in amori
la cui dolcezza ancora mi fa piangere ...
Tra i libri sparsi, pochi fiori

azzurrini, e l'erba, l'erba candida
tra le saggine, io davo a Cristo
tutta la mia ingenuità e il mio sangue.

Cantavano gli uccelli nel pulviscolo
in una trama complicata, incerta,
assordante, prede dell'esistere,

povere passioni perse tra i vertici
umili dei gelseti e dei sambuchi:
e io, come loro, nei luoghi deserti

destinati ai candidi, ai perduti,
aspettavo che scendesse la sera,
che si sentissero intorno i muti

odori del fuoco, della lieta miseria,
che l'Angelus suonasse, velato
del nuovo, contadino mistero

nell'antico mistero consumato.

Fu una breve passione. Erano servi
quei padri e quei figli che le sere
di Casarsa vivevano, così acerbi,

per me, di religione: le severe
loro allegrezze erano il grigiore
di chi, pur poco, ma possiede;

of the Tagliamento, were at the center
of earth and heaven; and there,
my throat, heart, and belly torn

on the distant path to the quarries,
I was consuming the hours of the most
beautiful human time, my whole

day of youth, in loves whose
sweetness still makes me weep . . .
Among scattered books, a few pale blue

flowers, and grass, in the pure grass
and heather, I was giving Christ all
my life's blood, all my innocence.

The birds were singing in the sunbeams
in an intricate uncertain weft,
deafening, vulnerable to existence,

poor passions lost among the humble
tops of mulberry groves and elders;
and I, like them, in those deserted places

destined for the honest and the lost,
was waiting for evening to fall,
for the silent smells of fire, for joyful

misery to be heard all around,
for the Angelus to sound,
veiled by the new, peasant mystery

rooted in the ancient mystery.

It was a brief passion. Those servants,
those fathers and sons living
the evenings of Casarsa, were, to me,

still untouched by religion; their severe
gaiety wore grey like those who
have little, but have at least something;

la chiesa del mio adolescente amore
era morta nei secoli, e vivente
solo nel vecchio, doloroso odore

dei campi. Spazzò la Resistenza
con nuovi sogni il sogno delle Regioni
Federate in Cristo, e il dolceardente

suo usignolo . . . Nessuna delle passioni
vere dell'uomo si rivelò
nelle parole e nelle azioni

della Chiesa. Anzi, guai a chi non può
non essere ad essa nuovo! Non dare
ad essa ingenuo tutto ciò

che in lui ondeggia come un mare
di troppo trepidante amore.
Guai a chi con gioia vitale

vuole servire una legge ch'è dolore!
Guai a chi con vitale dolore
si dona a una causa che nulla vuole

se non difendere la poca fede ancora
rimasta a dar rassegnazione al mondo!
Guai a chi crede che all'impeto del cuore

debba l'impeto della ragione rispondere!
Guai a chi non sa essere misero
nel misurare nell'anima i fondi

piani dell'egoismo e le derise
pazzie della pietà! Guai a chi crede
che la storia ad una eterna origine

—per candore piuttosto che per fede—
si sia interrotta, come il sole
del sogno; e non sa che è erede

the church of my adolescent love,
dead deep in the centuries, lived
only in the old dolorous odor

of the fields. The Resistance swept away
with new dreams the dream of the regions
federated in Christ and its sweetly burning

nightingale . . . None of man's true
passions were reflected
in the Church's words and deeds.

Indeed, woe to him who comes
to It for the first time, who
naïvely gives It everything

undulating in him like
a sea of trembling love.
Woe to him who filled with vital joy

desires to serve a law that's only sorrow!
Woe to him who filled with vital sorrow
gives himself to a cause whose only aim

is to defend what little remains of faith
and so give resignation to the world!
Woe to him who believes reason's impulse

should answer the heart's!
Woe to him who can't be miserly
when measuring the soul's deep

levels of egoism and its ridiculed
follies of pitying! Woe to him who believes
—more through innocence than faith—

that history at its eternal beginning
stood still, like the sun
in the dream; and doesn't know the Church

la Chiesa di ogni secolo creatore,
a difenderne gli istituiti beni,
l'orribile, animale grigiore

che vince nell'uomo luce e tenebra!
Guai a chi non sa che è borghese
questa fede cristiana, nel segno

di ogni privilegio, di ogni resa,
di ogni servitù; che il peccato
altro non è che reato di lesa

certezza quotidiana, odiato
per paura e aridità; che la Chiesa
è lo spietato cuore dello Stato.

                    *

Poveri, allegri cristi quattordicenni,
i due ragazzi di Donna Olimpia
possono buttare il loro giorno, pieni

di passione nella miscredenza, limpidi
nella confusione: possono andare
trascinati da quel povero impeto

del loro cuore quasi animale,
alle gioie mattutine di Villa Sciarra
e del Gianicolo, gioie di studenti, balie,

giovinette, verso la gazzarra
dei loro pari, che il solicello assorbe
in un patito alone d'erba e d'aria . . .

Mattine di pura vita! Quando sorde
sono le anime a ogni richiamo
che non sia quello del dolce disordine

del male e del bene quotidiano . . .
Essi lo vivono, abbandonati
da tutti, liberi in quel loro umano

is heir to each creating century;
and this awful animal greyness,
which defeats man's light and darkness,

defends Its corporate goods!
Woe to him who doesn't know
this Christian faith is bourgeois,

in every privilege, every rendering,
every servitude; that sin is
only a crime against offended

daily certitude, is hated because of
fear and sterility; that the Church
is the merciless heart of the State.

　　　*

Poor, joyous fourteen-year-old Christs,
the two boys from Donna Olimpia
can toss their whole day away,

passionately misbelieving,
lucidly confused,
drawn by their nearly animal

hearts' poor impulses toward
the morning joys of Villa Sciarra
and the Janiculum, joys of students, nurses,

young girls, toward the clamor their
friends make, which the pale sun absorbs
in a sickly halo of grass and air . . .

Mornings of pure life! When the soul
hears no other calls
than those of the sweet chaos

of daily good and evil . . .
They live it, abandoned
by all, free in their human fervor,

fervore a cui sono leggermente nati,
perché poveri, perché figli di poveri,
nel loro destino rassegnati

eppure sempre pronti alle nuove
avventure del sogno, che scendendo
dall'alto del mondo, li muove,

ingenui, e a cui essi corrotti si vendono,
benché nessuno li paghi: stracciati
ed eleganti al modo stupendo

dei romani, se ne vanno tra gli agiati
quartieri della gente per cui è vero il sogno . . .
Anche loro disadorni, ignorati,

a tenersi in cuore il loro bisogno
dell'accorante superfluo—seppure,
ormai, non d'altra classe ma d'altra nazione—

rivedo con le larghe e dure
facce contadine, l'occhio bruciante
di celeste, le tozze e sicure

membra di atleti dalle basse anche,
altri adolescenti . . . Sono, i loro calzoni,
sgraziati e quasi goffi, inelegante

il barbaro taglio delle loro chiome,
rasati alle tempie e alle nuche, e alti
i ciuffi disordinati, come

creste di guerra, piume di falchi.
Sono attenti, modesti: non sanno
incredulità, ironia, ma arsi

hanno gli sguardi da un affanno
e da un pudore che mettono a nudo
sempre nelle loro pupille la loro anima:

to which they were lightly born, because
poor, because sons of the poor,
resigned to their destiny and yet

always ready for new adventures
of the dream, which, descending from
the heights of the world, sets them innocently

in motion, and to which, corrupted, they sell
themselves, though no one pays them; tattered
and elegant in the marvelous manner of Romans,

they wander into the well-to-do
neighborhoods of people who live the dream . . .
And once more I see them: other adolescents,

also unadorned, unknown, though now
not from a different class but rather
from another nation, cherishing their need

for the heartrending superfluous, with their
wide tough peasant faces,
fiery pale blue eyes, low-hipped

stocky confident athletes'
limbs . . . Their trousers are
graceless, almost awkward, their barbarous

inelegant haircuts are shaved
at the temples and nape, with high
disorderly forelocks, like

war crests or hawk feathers.
They're modest, alert, innocent
of incredulity or irony, but

their eyes burn with an eagerness
and sense of decency that always
reveal their souls in their pupils,

tanto che non sai se all'inquietudine
di quelle anime l'aria è così nuova
e così chiara, o al vento che schiude

sopra quel loro mondo giovane
il vecchio odore dell'Asia . . .
Un vento che pare si muova

solo nel cielo intento nella pace
dell'immensità: e sull'immensa
città, spanda soltanto qualche lacero

soffio, come un misterioso incenso.
Sopra la Moscova il duomo
di San Basilio, sul grigio pavimento,

erige come un ragno d'oro addome
ed elitre, senza ormai vita.
Nell'altro estremo della piazza, come

a folle distanza, l'arrugginita
massa del Maneggio, cotta da un Dio
Settecentesco, un po' russo, un po' semita,

un po' tedesco . . . E dentro il pio
pallore della notte, le muraglie
del Cremlino chiudono al turbinio

della folla, sotto mute luminarie,
guglie e cupolette, ignote
oggi ancora agli occhi proletari . . .

Migliaia e migliaia di felici gote
di ragazzi la luce della Piazza Rossa
accende, raccolti in cerchi, in ruote,

in file, in quell'immensa fossa
su cui gli astri splendono vicini:
giocano, con semplice e commossa

so you don't know if the air
is made so new and clear by their
restless souls or by the wind

spreading Asia's old odor
over their young world . . .
A wind that seems to move

alone in the sky immersed in the peace
of the immensity; and over the immense
city, only a few tattered breezes seem

to spread, like some mysterious incense.
Above the Moscova, the cathedral
of Saint Basil, on its grey floor,

like a golden spider, erects by now
lifeless abdomen and elytra.
At another corner of the square

as though at an insane distance, the rusted
mass of the Manège, baked by an eighteenth-
century God, slightly Russian, part Semitic,

a bit German . . . And in the pious
whiteness of the night, the Kremlin
walls are closed to the swirling

crowd, under silent luminations,
spires, and little cupolas, unseen
even today by proletarian eyes . . .

Thousands on thousands of joyous cheeks of boys,
which the light of Red Square brightens,
gathering in circles, wheels, lines,

in that immense ditch over which,
so close to earth, the stars shine;
they play, with simple excited joy

gioia, come—sotto gli scalini
della chiesa, nella loro piazzetta—
gli ingenui ragazzi contadini.

Si tengono per mano in una stretta
rozza e affettuosa, file di maschi,
circondando qualche giovinetta;

altri, più giovani, intorno, rimasti
senza gioco, si spingono violenti
a guardare coi cupi, casti

occhi, qualcuno che tenti
un passo di danza, alla pura e folta
musica dei primitivi strumenti.

Una marea di girotondi lungo la svolta
della muraglia . . . Sono questi i figli
della fame, i figli della rivolta,

i figli del sangue, sono questi i figli
dei pionieri che hanno solo lottato,
degli eroi senza nome, i figli

del lontano futuro disperato!
Eccoli sul mondo, ora: e del mondo
padroni. E il mondo no, non è beato

per loro, benché umilmente giocondo
lo guardi il loro occhio: poco
più veste la loro gioventù che il biondo

capo, l'interna forza, il fuoco
del pudore, per le enormi vie, gli enormi
casamenti, stesi sopra il vuoto

della città potente e senza forma,
che accoglie le loro nuove vite.
Ma è religioso l'ardore di cui colme

like innocent peasant boys
at the foot of the steps of
a church in a village square.

Lines of males hold hands
roughly, affectionately,
circling a young girl;

others, younger, scattering, excluded
from the game, push ahead, violent,
to look with dark chaste

eyes at someone attempting
a dance step to the primitive
instruments' pure thick music.

A tide of ring-around-a-rose along
the bending walls . . . These are the sons
of hunger, the sons of revolt,

the sons of blood, these the sons
of always-struggling pioneers,
of nameless heroes, sons

of the distant desperate future!
Here they are now in the world, and of the world:
masters. But the world isn't blessèd

to them, though they look
at it with humble joy; their youth possesses
little more than their blond

heads, inward strength, and fire
of decency, along the enormous streets
and blocks stretching over the void

of the potent formless city, which receives
their new lives. But it is with religious
fire that, swelling, almost blind

e quasi cieche alle pupille ardite,
come a donarsi o a testimoniarsi,
tremano le loro anime amiche.

*

Questi due che per quartieri sparsi
di luce e miseria, vanno abbracciati,
lieti paganamente dei loro passi,

dicono con faccia lieta che mille facce
ha la storia, e che spesso chi è indietro
è primo: così chiaramente incarnate

sono nel loro ingenuo petto
le confuse e reali speranze del mondo,
che possono ogni atto anche abbietto,

ogni miscredenza, ogni inverecondia . . .

Ma noi? Ah, certo, c'è in ogni errore un lievito
di verità: può essere libero e limpido
ogni occhio più servo e opaco, a ricevere

la vita esterna, non solo per gli istinti
stupenda perché esiste, ma anche
per il pensiero, che ne assiste—vinto,

sia pure, e impotente—l'esaltante
pluralità, la magica stranezza
vivace, le misteriose mescolanze

di grande e povero, l'abbietta
luce e l'eletta incoscienza.
Pietà per la creatura! Ad essa,

a questa pietà spietata, e senza
religione, basta qualunque religione,
anche la cattolica, se un'Esistenza

in their bold pupils, as though to give
of themselves or bear witness to themselves,
their friendly souls tremble.

*

These two moving arm in arm through neighborhoods
of alternating light and poverty, rejoicing
like pagans in their footsteps' sound,

are saying, with a joyous face, that history
has a thousand faces, that the last is
often first: So clearly incarnated

in their innocent breasts are the world's
confused and real hopes, that they're
capable of any act, even a base one,

any false belief, any indecency . . .

As for us—of course, in every error there's
a seed of truth: Every eye, even the most servile
and opaque, can be free and limpid for receiving

external life, miraculous because
it exists for the instincts
as well as for thought, which—though

defeated and powerless—witnesses
the exalting variety, vivacious
magic strangeness, mysterious mixtures

of great and poor, lowly
light and intentional unawareness.
Pity the creatures: As for

this pitiless, religionless
pity, any religion suffices,
even the Catholic, if it instills

magicamente diversa pone
nel fondo di quella creatura
stravagante nel vero, alone

che la divora, sia essa dura
per interna paura, tenera
per una nuova, oscura

volontà di esistere, sia essa degenere
o pura, venduta o santa,
eslege o umilmente perbene:

una delle infinite branche della pianta
che frondeggia alla semplice vita,
in città, borgate, tuguri, ponti, antri,

amica nella sua esistenza nemica,
allegra nell'ingiustizia antica,
urlante nell'amore che mendica.

Sì, certo, quanto scolorita,
se reale, può apparire la greggia
che vive, a chi con quella pietà divertita

e sacrilega vi guardi brillare la scheggia
del divino! E consideri divina,
dentro la propria anima attenta, la legge

di un ambiguo, disperato destino:
l'egoismo, la mistificazione,
il capriccio e la durezza del bambino.

Io, bambino in altro modo, per la passione,
e spinto per questo ad essere uomo
con tutto il suo sapore d'umile convenzione

(da cui ingenuamente sono
costretto a essere sempre chiaro
in ogni rapporto, e, per condanna, buono)

a magically different existence
in the depths of those
extravagant creatures, halo

that devours them, whether they're
tough because of inward fear or
tender because of a new obscure

will to exist, degenerate
or pure, corrupted or saintly,
outlaw or humbly respectable:

any of the infinite branches of the plant
that sprouts leaves of simple life,
in cities, slums, hovels, caves, on bridges,

a friend in their hostile existence,
joyful amid ancient injustice,
shouting the love they beg for.

Yes, of course, how colorless though
real the living herd can seem
to one who, with amused sacrilegious

pity, looks at the fragment of the divine
shining in it! And within his own
attentive soul considers divine the law

of an ambiguous desperate destiny:
a child's egoism, whims,
mystifications, and toughness.

I, child in a different way, through passion,
and forced because of this to be a man
with all his airs of humble convention

(which always obligate me,
innocently, to be clear in every
relationship and condemn me to be good)

mi sforzo a capire ogni cosa, ignaro
come sono d'altra vita che non sia
la mia, fino perdutamente a fare

di altra vita, nella nostalgia,
piena esperienza: sono tutto pietà,
ma voglio che diversa sia la via

del mio amore per questa realtà,
che anch'io amerei caso per caso, creatura
per creatura. Mi voglio diverso: ma

ahi, come so capire coloro che tale figura
dell'anima siano spinti a esprimere!
Col più alto di questi, andavo per l'oscura

galleria dei viali, una notte, al confine
della città, battuta dalle anime
perdute, sporchi crocefissi senza spine,

allegri e feroci, ragazzacci e mondane,
presi da ire di viscere, da gioie
leggere come le brezze lontane

scorrenti su loro, su noi,
dal mare ai colli, nel tempo
delle notti che mai non muoiono . . .

Io sentivo il sacrilego sentimento
che esaltava il mio amico a quelle
forme dell'esistere, prede d'un vento

che le trascinava sulla terra,
senza vita alla morte, senza coscienza
alla luce: ma gli erano sorelle:

come per lui, lottare per l'esistenza
fu buio in cuore, male, disprezzo
vitale per l'esistenza altrui, adolescenza

I force myself to understand everything,
ignorant as I am of any life that isn't
mine, till, desperate in my nostalgia,

I realize the full experience
of another life; I'm all compassion,
but I wish the road of my love for

this reality would be different, that I
then would love individuals, one by one.
I want to be different, but alas

how well I understand those driven to
express this particular form of the soul!
One night with one of the best of them,

I walked the dark tunnel of the boulevards,
at the edge of the city, cruised by lost
souls, uncrowned dirty crucifixes,

punks laughing, wild, and whores
seized by gut furies and by joys
light as distant breezes

streaming over them, over us,
from the sea to the hills in the time
of nights that never die . . .

I was sharing the sacrilegious feeling
that made my friend celebrate those
forms of existence, victims of a wind

dragging them over the earth, lifeless
toward death, unaware toward
the light, but who were his sisters:

for them as for him, the struggle to live
meant a darkened heart, a living evil
contempt for others' lives, humiliating

umiliante, e felice, in mezzo
al branco dei lupi ben adulti,
loro sì, pronti, aggiornati sul prezzo

della vita: custodi di culti
o padroni di stati, ladri o servi,
arrivisti o autorità, re o ultimi

dei paria, tutti, fino dai più acerbi
anni, nella norma che vuole uguali:
a non capire, a capire senza mai perdersi.

Poi corremmo come in cerca dell'ignaro
Dio che li animava: lui lo sapeva, dove.
Guidava la sua Cadillac di cinematografaro,

con un dito, arruffando con l'altro la giovane
sua grossa testa, parlando, stanco e instancabile . . .
Giungemmo: dietro a Tor Vajanica,

un vento inaspettato, ora, soffiava:
le file dei capanni, sgangherate, come
rottami, con spruzzi di calce, e la cava

schiena, il biancheggiante addome
d'una barca, erano soli a resistergli.
Due giovinetti, rimasti senza nome,

ci pedinarono un po', senza insistere,
in qualche loro sordida, calda speranza.
Bruni e tremanti sparvero. E miste

alle spume, all'acqua, lì vicina—tanta
quanta in una pozza di temporale,
nella tenebra di qualche infanzia—

ecco la luce e la bianchezza immortale
del Dio: dritto, vicino, che col fiato
ci bagnava, dall'arruffato mare,

adolescence, happy now among the
other full-grown wolves,
sure of life's latest quoted

price: custodians of cults or chiefs
of state, thieves or slaves, arrivistes
or authorities, kings or the last pariahs,

all, from their earliest days, under the law
that wants all to be equals: without understanding
or understanding without ever losing oneself.

Then off we went, in search of the ignorant
God that animated them: he knew where it was.
He was driving his film-director's Cadillac

with one finger, ruffling with another his
young big head, talking, tired, untiring . . .
We got there. Behind Tor Vajanica

there was a sudden unexpected wind
resisted only by the rows of
dilapidated cabañas, like ruins splashed

with whitewash, and the curved back
and whitening abdomen of a boat.
Two young boys, who remained anonymous,

followed us for a bit, though not insisting
on some warm sordid hope of theirs.
Tanned, shivering, they soon disappeared. And mixing

with the nearby foam and water—as though
in a puddle from a thunderstorm
in the darkness of some childhood—

there was the sudden light and immortal whiteness
of the God: erect, close by, wetting us
with his breath, out of the disheveled sea,

in una colonna salata ed estatica
di pulviscolo, così violento al tatto,
che il rombo del frangente s'era smorzato.

. . . .

*

Sì, certo, era un Dio . . . e altri meno pazzi
e stupendi ce n'è. Coi loro sacerdoti,
e, vorrei anche dire, con i loro santi.

Santi poveri, martoriati dai ben noti
dolori, col terribile dovere
di arrivare, senza troppi terremoti,

alla fine del mese per riavere
in tasca le poche sospirate lire:
impiegatucci, funzionari, leve

di un Partito, per cui vivere e morire.
Felici ti mostrano un paio di scarpe
nuove, un quadruccio buono all'appena civile

parete della casa, una bella sciarpa
natalizia per la moglie: ma dentro,
dietro quell'infantile palpito,

quello stento, ti misurano col metro
della loro fede, del loro sacrificio.
Sono inflessibili, sono tetri,

nel loro giudicarti: chi ha il cilicio
addosso non può perdonare.
Non puoi da loro aspettare una briciola

di pietà: non perché lo insegni Marx,
ma per quel loro dio d'amore,
elementare vittoria di bene sul male,

in a salty ecstatic column of light
particles so violent to the touch
the breakers' roars were muffled.

. . . .

　　*

Yes, certainly it was a God . . . and there are others
less mad and amazing. With their priests
and, I might even say, their saints.

Poor saints, martyred by common
sorrows and the terrible duty
of arriving at the end of the month

without too many disasters, to retrieve
their few precious liras:
petty clerks, functionaries, recruits

of a Party to give one's life for and to.
Happy to show you their new shoes,
a little painting just right for their

barely decorated walls, or a nice
Christmas scarf for the wife; but deep
inside behind that childishness

and hardships, they're measuring you with
the rule of their faith and sacrifice.
Inflexible and grim, they

judge you; those in
hairshirts can't forgive.
You can't expect even a crumb of mercy

from them: not because Marx teaches it,
but because of their god of love, elementary
victory of good over evil, which informs

ch'è nei loro atti. Ma come nel biancore
dell'estetico dio del mare, informe Forma,
mescolanza irrazionale di gioia e dolore,

sbianca l'opacità del gesso, la norma
che svaluta . . . così arrossa nel rosso
dell'altro Dio—quello che trasforma

il mondo, quello futuro ed incorrotto—
il sangue dei giorni di Stalin . . .
Non torna nulla. Nemmeno il paradosso

esistenziale, in cui, fertili-aridi,
vivono quasi tutti coloro che conosco:
borghesi colti, esperti di essenziali

infrastrutture, spiriti del bosco
della mondanità, della cultura:
a popolare le pure sere di Piazza del Popolo,

dei nuovi quartieri oltre le vecchie mura,
del centro dove la città s'infossa
in preziosi vicoli scintillanti e luridi . . .

Genio arreso, con le sue quattro ossa
sotto eleganti vesti, ognuno porta intorno
una faccia intenta, dove gli altri possano

sospettare qualcosa; nei caffè, di giorno,
nei salotti, la sera: ma ognuno cerca
nella faccia dell'altro invano un ritorno

delle speranze antiche: e se vi accerta
una speranza, è una speranza inconfessabile,
nel cerchio della domanda e dell'offerta,

il cui sguardo è come per uno spasimo
di interna ferita: che rende esanimi,
accidiosi, scontenti, spinge a uno sciopero

everything they do. But just as the whiteness
of the beautiful god of the sea, formless Form,
irrational mix of joy and sorrow,

bleaches the opacity of plaster, the norm
that devalues . . . so too the blood of Stalin's days
turns redder in the red of that other

God, that future uncorrupted
world-transforming God . . .
Nothing works out anymore. Not even the existential

paradox, in which almost everyone I
know lives, fertile-sterile:
cultivated bourgeois, experts of essential

infrastructures, spirits of the wood
of worldliness and culture who populate
the pure evenings of Piazza del Popolo,

the new neighborhoods beyond the old walls,
the center where Rome clogs up with
precious sparkling lurid alleyways . . .

The sold-out genius has bones beneath
his elegant clothes; everyone's face
is intense, so others might suspect

something, in cafés by day, salons
after dark; but each vainly searches
others' faces for a return

of the ancient hopes; and if he detects
a hope there, it's unconfessable
in the circle of supply and demand,

its look seems caused by the spasm
of an internal wound, making one lifeless,
slothful, discontented, driving one to a strike

dei sentimenti, a una colpevole stasi
della coscienza, ad una pace insana,
che vuole i nostri giorni grigi e tragici.

Così, se guardo in fondo alle anime
delle schiere di individui vivi
nel mio tempo, a me vicini o non lontani,

vedo che dei mille sacrilegi possibili
che ogni religione naturale
può enumerare, quello che rimane

sempre, in tutti, è la viltà.
Un sentimento eterno—una forma
del sentimento—fossile, immutabile,

che lascia in ogni altro sentimento
diretta o indiretta, la sua orma.
È quella viltà che fa l'uomo irreligioso.

È come un profondo impedimento
che, all'uomo, toglie forza al cuore,
calore al ragionamento,

che lo fa ragionare di bontà
come di un puro comportamento,
di pietà come di una pura norma.

Può renderlo feroce, qualche volta,
ma sempre lo rende prudente:
minaccia, giudica, ironizza, ascolta,

ma è sempre, interiormente, impaurito.
Non c'è nessuno che sfugga a questa paura.
Nessuno perciò è davvero amico o nemico.

Nessuno sa sentire vera passione:
ogni sua luce subito s'oscura
come per rassegnazione o pentimento

of feelings, a guilty stasis
of conscience, an insane peace
when our days must be grey and tragic.

If I look deep into the souls
of the hosts of individuals living
in my time, friend or neighbor,

I see, of the thousand possible
sacrileges each natural religion
forbids, the one that remains in all

people always is cowardice.
An eternal feeling—a form
of feeling—immutable fossil

which impresses on every other feeling
direct or indirect traces of itself.
It's that cowardice which makes man irreligious.

It's like a profound impediment
that takes away from him his strength
of heart and warmth of reasoning

and makes him reason about goodness
as though it were behavioral,
about compassion as though it were the rule.

Although it can render him ferocious
sometimes, it always makes him prudent;
though he threatens, judges, listens, mocks,

deep down he's always afraid.
No one escapes this fear. Thus
no one's really friend or enemy.

No one knows how to feel true passion;
all its brightness immediately dims
as though from resignation or repentance,

in quella antica viltà, in quell'ormone
misterioso che si è formato nei secoli.
Lo riconosco, sempre, in ogni uomo.

Lo so bene che altro non è che insicurezza
vitale, antica angoscia economica:
che era regola della nostra vita animale

ed è stata assimilata ora in queste povere
nostre comunità: che è difesa,
disperata, che si annida là dove

c'è un minimo di pace: nel possesso.
E ogni possesso è uguale: dall'industria
al campicello, dalla nave al carretto.

Perciò è uguale in tutti la viltà:
com'è alle grige origini o agli ultimi
grigi giorni di ogni civiltà . . .

Così la mia nazione è ritornata al punto
di partenza, nel ricorso dell'empietà.
E, chi non crede in nulla, ne ha coscienza,

e la governa. Non ha certo rimorso,
chi non crede in nulla, ed è cattolico,
a saper d'essere spietatamente in torto.

Usando nei ricatti e i disonori
quotidiani sicari provinciali,
volgari fin nel più profondo del cuore,

vuole uccidere ogni forma di religione,
nell'irreligioso pretesto di difenderla:
vuole, in nome d'un Dio morto, essere padrone.

Qui, tra le case, le piazze, le strade piene
di bassezza, della città in cui domina
ormai questo nuovo spirito che offende

in that ancient cowardice, in that
mysterious hormone formed through centuries.
I recognize it always in every man.

I know it's really only insecurity
about life, ancient economic anxiety;
that it was the rule of our animal life

and now has been assimilated into
these poor communities of ours; that it's
a desperate defense and nests where

there's a minimum of peace, in possessions.
And all possessions are alike: whether
industry or pasture, ship or pushcart. Thus

cowardice is the same in everyone:
the same in the grey beginnings or the last
grey days of every civilization . . .

And so my country's come full circle
in the recurrence of wickedness.
And those who believe in nothing understand

the situation and govern. They feel no remorse,
unbelieving but still Catholic,
even if they know they're mercilessly wrong.

Using profoundly vulgar
provincial killers for their
putrid deals and daily blackmail,

they desire to kill all religion
on the irreligious pretext of defending it
and rule in the name of a dead God.

Here, in the mean streets, squares,
and houses of the city that
this new spirit now dominates, which

l'anima ad ogni istante,—con i duomi,
le chiese, i monumenti muti nel disuso
angoscioso che è l'uso d'uomini

che non credono—io mi ricuso
ormai a vivere. Non c'è più niente
oltre la natura—in cui del resto è effuso

solo il fascino della morte—niente
di questo mondo umano che io ami.
Tutto mi dà dolore: questa gente

che segue supina ogni richiamo
da cui i suoi padroni la vogliono chiamata,
adottando, sbadata, le più infami

abitudini di vittima predestinata;
il grigio dei suoi vestiti per le grige strade;
i suoi grigi gesti in cui sembra stampata

l'omertà del male che l'invade;
il suo brulicare intorno a un benessere
illusorio, come un gregge intorno a poche biade;

la sua regolarità di marea, per cui resse
e deserti si alternano per le vie,
ordinati da flussi e da riflussi ossessi

e anonimi di necessità stantie;
i suoi sciami ai tetri bar, ai tetri cinema,
il cuore tetramente arreso al quia . . .

E intorno a questo interno dominio
della volgarità, la città che si sgretola
ammucchiandosi, brasiliana o levantina,

come l'espansione di una lebbra
che si bea ebbra di morte sugli strati
dell'epoche umane, cristiane o greche,

constantly insults the soul—cathedrals,
churches, and monuments silent in
the anguished disuse that is the use

of those who don't believe—here I now
refuse to live. Nothing remains
but nature—which, though, emits

only the fascination of death—nothing
in this human world I love.
Everything grieves me: this passive

people following every call
by which their masters wish them called,
carelessly adopting the most infamous

habits of predestined victims:
grey clothes in grey streets;
grey gestures stamped by their

complicity with the evil that's invaded them;
swarming around an illusion of
affluence, like a herd at its oats;

their tidal regularity, through which crowds
and deserts alternate along streets
arranged by obsessed anonymous

ebbs and flows of stale necessity;
swarms of them at gloomy cafés and cinemas,
hearts gloomily surrendered to reason . . .

And around this inner dominion
of vulgarity, the city crumbles
into rubble—Brazilian or Levantine,

as though from a voracious leprosy
that, drunk with death, delights on layers
of human eras, Christian, Greek—

e allinea tempeste di caseggiati,
gore di lotti color bile o vomito,
senza senso, né di affanno né di pace;

sradica i riposanti muri, i gomiti
poetici dei vicoli sui giardini interni,
i superstiti casolari dalla tinta di pomice

o topo, tra cui fichi, radicchi, svernano
beati, i selciati striati di una grama
erbetta, i rioni che parevano eterni

nei loro lineamenti quasi umani
di grigio mattone o smunto cotto:
tutto distrugge la volgare fiumana

dei pii possessori di lotti:
questi cuori di cani, questi occhi profanatori,
questi turpi alunni di un Gesù corrotto

nei salotti vaticani, negli oratori,
nelle anticamere dei ministri, nei pulpiti:
forti di un popolo di servitori.

Com'è giunto lontano dai tumulti
puramente interiori del suo cuore,
e dal paesaggio di primule e virgulti

del materno Friuli, l'Usignolo
dolceardente della Chiesa Cattolica!
Il suo sacrilego, ma religioso amore

non è più che un ricordo, un'ars retorica:
ma è lui, che è morto, non io, d'ira,
d'amore deluso, di ansia spasmodica

per una tradizione che è uccisa
ogni giorno da chi se ne vuole difensore;
e con lui è morta una terra arrisa

puts storms of city blocks next to swampy
vacant lots the color of vomit or bile
with no feeling for either anxiety or peace;

uproots serene walls, poetic elbows
of lanes in interior gardens, the few surviving
farmhouses the color of mice or pumice

where fig trees and chicory blissfully
winter, cobblestones striped by dismal
weeds, neighborhoods that looked eternal

in their almost human lineaments
of grey brick, pale brickwork;
all destroyed by the vulgar

torrent of pious landlords with
dog hearts and profaning eyes,
vile disciples of a Jesus corrupted

in the Vatican's salons and Sunday schools,
priests' waiting rooms and pulpits:
strong over a people of serfs.

How far it has come, the sweetly
burning Nightingale of the Catholic Church,
from the purely inward turmoil

of its heart, how far from the bush
and primrose landscape of Mother Friuli!
Its sacrilegious but religious love

is only a memory now, an *ars retorica*:
but it's what died, not I, of anger
and unrequited love, of spasmodic anxiety

for a tradition daily murdered
by those who pretend to defend it;
and dead too, a land blessed

da religiosa luce, col suo nitore
contadino di campi e casolari;
è morta una madre ch'è mitezza e candore

mai turbati in un tempo di solo male;
ed è morta un'epoca della nostra esistenza,
che in un mondo destinato a umiliare

fu luce morale e resistenza.

    (1957)

by religious light, with its peasant
neatness of fields and farmhouses;
and dead a mother all meekness and purity

unchangeable even in a time of total evil;
and dead an epoch of our existence,
which in a world destined to humiliate us

was moral light and resistance.

(1957)

Pur sopravvivendo, in una lunga appendice
di inesausta, inesauribile passione
—che quasi in un altro tempo ha la radice—

so che una luce, nel caos, di religione,
una luce di bene, mi redime
il troppo amore nella disperazione . . .

È una povera donna, mite, fine,
che non ha quasi coraggio di essere,
e se ne sta nell'ombra, come una bambina,

coi suoi radi capelli, le sue vesti dimesse,
ormai, e quasi povere, su quei sopravvissuti
segreti che sanno, ancora, di violette;

con la sua forza, adoperata nei muti
affanni di chi teme di non essere pari
al dovere, e non si lamenta dei mai avuti

compensi: una povera donna che sa amare
soltanto, eroicamente, ed essere madre
è stato per lei tutto ciò che si può dare.

La casa è piena delle sue magre
membra di bambina, della sua fatica:
anche a notte, nel sonno, asciutte lacrime

coprono ogni cosa: e una pietà così antica,
così tremenda mi stringe il cuore,
rincasando, che urlerei, mi toglierei la vita.

Tutto intorno ferocemente muore,
mentre non muore il bene che è in lei,
e non sa quanto il suo umile amore,

In a long appendix of unexhausted,
inexhaustible passion, which seems to
have come from another age, I'm surviving,

and I know, in the chaos, a light, of religion,
a light of good, redeems
my desperate excessive love . . .

It's a poor, meek, sweet woman,
who has barely the courage to live,
and stays in the shadows like a child;

with her thin hair, her by-now modest
almost poor clothes, her surviving
still violet-scented secrets;

her strength employed in the silent anxieties
of those afraid of being unequal to their
duty, who don't complain about never receiving

their just rewards: a poor woman who knows
only how to love, heroically; and being
a mother has been the greatest gift.

The house is filled with her frail
childlike limbs and her labors;
even at night, as she sleeps, dry weeping

covers everything; and such a terrible ancient
pity grips my heart, returning home,
I could scream, I could take my life.

Everything all around her ferociously dies
but the good within her doesn't die
and she doesn't know how much her humble love

—poveri, dolci ossimini miei—
possano nel confronto quasi farmi morire
di dolore e vergogna, quanto quei

suoi gesti angustiati, quei suoi sospiri
nel silenzio della nostra cucina,
possano farmi apparire impuro e vile . . .

In ogni ora, tutto è ormai, per lei, bambina,
per me, suo figlio, e da sempre, finito:
non resta che sperare che la fine

venga davvero a spegnere l'accanito
dolore di aspettarla. Saremo insieme,
presto, in quel povero prato gremito

di pietre grige, dove fresco il seme
dell'esistenza dà ogni anno erbe e fiori:
nient'altro ormai che la campagna preme

ai suoi confini di muretti, tra i voli
delle allodole, a giorno, e a notte,
il canto disperato degli usignoli.

Farfalle e insetti ce n'è a frotte,
fino al tardo settembre, la stagione
in cui torniamo, lì dove le ossa

dell'altro figlio tiene la passione
ancora vive nel gelo della pace:
vi arriva, ogni pomeriggio, depone

i suoi fiori, in ordine, mentre tutto tace
intorno, e si sente solo il suo affanno,
pulisce la pietra, dove, ansioso, lui giace,

poi si allontana, e nel silenzio che hanno
subito ritrovato intorno muri e solchi,
si sentono i tonfi della pompa che tremando

—poor sweet little bones I love—
by comparison makes me almost die
of grief and shame, how much her

anguished gestures, her sighing
in the silence of our kitchen,
can make me seem impure and cowardly . . .

Each moment, for her, child that she is, and for
me, her son, and forever—everything's finished:
nothing remains but to hope the end

will come to extinguish the unrelenting
pain of waiting for it. We'll be together,
soon, in that poor meadow crowded

with grey stones, where every year the fresh
seed of existence sends forth grass and flowers;
now only countryside presses at its

boundaries of low walls, among flights
of larks by day and in the dark
the desperate song of the nightingale.

Butterflies and other insects swarm
till late September, the season
when we go back there where passion

keeps alive the other son's
bones in icy peacetime;
every afternoon she comes

to arrange her flowers, while all around her
all is still, and one senses only her grief;
she cleans the stone he sleeps anxiously under,

then goes away, and in the silence that walls
and furrows immediately retrieve,
one hears the thudding pump she pushes,

lei spinge con le sue poche forze,
volonterosa, decisa a fare ciò che è bene:
e torna, attraversando le aiuole folte

di nuova erbetta, con quei suoi vasi pieni
d'acqua per quei fiori . . . Presto
anche noi, dolce superstite, saremo

perduti in fondo a questo fresco
pezzo di terra: ma non sarà una quiete
la nostra, ché si mescola in essa

troppo una vita che non ha avuto meta.
Avremo un silenzio stento e povero,
un sonno doloroso, che non reca

dolcezza e pace, ma nostalgia e rimprovero,
la tristezza di chi è morto senza vita:
se qualcosa di puro, e sempre giovane,

vi resterà, sarà il tuo mondo mite,
la tua fiducia, il tuo eroismo:
nella dolcezza del gelso e della vite

o del sambuco, in ogni alto o misero
segno di vita, in ogni primavera, sarai
tu; in ogni luogo dove un giorno risero,

e di nuovo ridono, impuri, i vivi, tu darai
la purezza, l'unico giudizio che ci avanza,
ed è tremendo, e dolce: ché non c'è mai

disperazione senza un po' di speranza.

trembling, with her feeble strength, full
of good will, determined to do what's right;
then she comes back, crossing flowerbeds thick

with new grass, carrying vases full
of water for those flowers . . . Soon
we too, sweet survivor, will be

lost at the bottom of this
cool plot of land; but we won't rest,
for mixed up in us is too much

a life without a goal.
We'll have a difficult silence,
a sorrowing sleep, which brings,

not sweetness and peace, but nostalgia and reproaches,
the sadness of those who die without living;
but if something pure and always young

remains, it will be your meek world,
your trust, your heroism:
in the sweetness of the mulberry, grapevine,

and elder, in every high or wretched
proof of life, in every spring, you'll be there;
in every place where once the impure living

laughed and once again will laugh, you'll bestow
the purity, the only judgment left us,
and it's terrible and sweet, for we never have

despair without some small hope.

POETRY
IN THE FORM
OF A ROSE

(1964)

PART THREE

È difficile dire con parole di figlio
ciò a cui nel cuore ben poco assomiglio.

Tu sei la sola al mondo che sa, del mio cuore,
ciò che è stato sempre, prima d'ogni altro amore.

Per questo devo dirti ciò ch'è orrendo conoscere:
è dentro la tua grazia che nasce la mia angoscia.

Sei insostituibile. Per questo è dannata
alla solitudine la vita che mi hai data.

E non voglio esser solo. Ho un'infinita fame
d'amore, dell'amore di corpi senza anima.

Perché l'anima è in te, sei tu, ma tu
sei mia madre e il tuo amore è la mia schiavitù:

ho passato l'infanzia schiavo di questo senso
alto, irrimediabile, di un impegno immenso.

Era l'unico modo per sentire la vita,
l'unica tinta, l'unica forma: ora è finita.

Sopravviviamo: ed è la confusione
di una vita rinata fuori dalla ragione.

Ti supplico, ah, ti supplico: non voler morire.
Sono qui, solo, con te, in un futuro aprile . . .

    (1962)

PRAYER TO MY MOTHER

It's so hard to say in a son's words
what I'm so little like in my heart.

Only you in all the world know what my
heart always held, before any other love.

So, I must tell you something terrible to know:
From within your kindness my anguish grew.

You're irreplaceable. And because you are,
the life you gave me is condemned to loneliness.

And I don't want to be alone. I have an infinite
hunger for love, love of bodies without souls.

For the soul is inside you, it is you, but
you're my mother and your love's my slavery:

My childhood I lived a slave to this lofty
incurable sense of an immense obligation.

It was the only way to feel life,
the unique form, sole color; now, it's over.

We survive, in the confusion
of a life reborn outside reason.

I pray you, oh, I pray: Don't die.
I'm here, alone, with you, in a future April . . .

    (1962)

Oh, fine pratico della mia poesia!
Per esso non so vincere l'ingenuità
che mi toglie prestigio, per esso la mia

lingua si crepa nell'ansietà
che io devo soffocare parlando.
Cerco, nel mio cuore, solo ciò che ha!

A questo mi son ridotto: quando
scrivo poesia è per difendermi e lottare,
compromettendomi, rinunciando

a ogni antica mia dignità: appare,
così, indifeso quel mio cuore elegiaco
di cui ho vergogna, e stanca e vitale

riflette la mia lingua una fantasia
di figlio che non sarà mai padre . . .
Pian piano intanto ho perso la mia compagnia

di poeti dalle faccie nude, aride,
di divine capre, con le fronti dure
dei padri padani, nelle cui magre

file contano soltanto le pure
relazioni di passione e pensiero.
Trascinato via dalle mie oscure

vicende. Ah, ricominciare da zero!
solo come un cadavere nella sua fossa!
E così, ecco questa mattina in cui non spero

che nella luce . . . Sì, nella luce che disossa
con la sua felicità primaverile
le giornate di questa mia Canossa.

Oh practical end of my poetry!
Because of you I can't overcome
the naïveté that shrivels my prestige;

because of you, my tongue cracks with
anxiety, which I have to smother with talk.
I search my heart only for what's there.

To this I'm reduced: when I write
poetry, it's to defend myself, to fight,
compromising myself, renouncing

all my ancient dignity; thus
my defenseless elegiac heart comes
to shame me; and tired, though alive,

my words reveal the fantasy
of the son who'll never be a father . . .
Meanwhile, one by one, I lost my poet

comrades with their naked wind-dried faces,
sacred goats like stern-faced
Po Valley fathers, in whose thin

ranks only pure relations of
passion and thought matter.
Carried along by the obscure events

of my life! Oh, to start again from scratch!
Alone like a cadaver in its grave!
Such a morning!—in which I hope

only in light . . . yes, in light
whose springtime joy cuts through
these days of my Canossa.

Eccomi nel chiarore di un vecchio aprile,
a confessarmi, inginocchiato,
fino in fondo, fino a morire.

Ci pensi questa luce a darmi fiato,
a reggere il filo con la sua biondezza
fragrante, su un mondo, come la morte, rinato.

Poi . . . ah, nel sole è la mia sola lietezza . . .
quei corpi, coi calzoni dell'estate,
un po' lisi nel grembo per la distratta carezza

di rozze mani impolverate . . . Le sudate
comitive di maschi adolescenti,
sui margini di prati, sotto facciate

di case, nei crepuscoli cocenti . . .
L'orgasmo della città festiva,
la pace delle campagne rifiorenti . . .

E loro, con le loro faccie vivide
o nere d'ombra, come di cuccioli lupi,
in pigre scorribande, in lascive

ingenuità . . . Quelle nuche! Quei cupi
sguardi! Quel bisogno di sorridere,
ora per i loro discorsi, un poco stupidi,

d'innocenti, ora come per sfida
al resto del mondo che li accoglie:
FIGLI. Ah, quale Dio li guida

così certi, qui lungo le strade più spoglie,
ai Castelli, alle Spiagge, alle Porte
della città, nelle previste, antiche voglie

di chi sa già che giungerà alla morte
dopo essere veramente vissuto:
che la vita che ha in sorte

Now here in the clear glow of an old April
I'm kneeling in confession
till the end of my life.

May this light give me breath,
may it unreel its fragrant golden thread
on a world, like death, reborn.

But oh . . . there in the sunlight's my sole delight . . .
those bodies, their summer trousers slightly
worn at the groin by unconscious caresses

of rough dusty hands . . . Sweaty
bands of teen-age males
at edges of fields, slouched

against façades in scorching dusks . . .
The festive city's orgasmic excitement,
the peaceful countryside flowering again . . .

And them, their faces vivid
or dark, shadowy, like wolf cubs,
in lazy forays, in lascivious

naïveté . . . Those napes! Those dark
glances! That need to smile
in their slightly stupid conversations

of the innocent, now like a challenge
to the rest of the world that receives them:
sons. Oh, what God guides them

so sure, along the barest roads,
to the Castelli, the beaches, the city's
gates in the predictable ancient desires

of him who is confident he'll arrive
at death only after truly living:
that the life that fell to his lot

è quella giusta, e nulla avrà perduto.
Umili, certo. E quello che sarà
il loro modo vile, poi, d'aver compiuto

se stessi (il loro destino è la viltà),
è ancora un albeggiare quasi
su sconosciuti alberi, in cui ha

la natura soltanto gemme, in una stasi
di purezza suprema, di coraggio.
Oh, certo, essi sono invasi

ormai dal male che ricevono in retaggio
dai padri—mia coetanea, nera razza.
Ma in che cosa sperano? che raggio

di luce li colpisce, in quella faccia
dove l'attaccatura dei capelli
alla fronte, i ciuffi, le onde sono grazia

più che corporea? . . . Dolcemente ribelli,
e, insieme, contenti del futuro dei padri:
ecco che cosa li fa così belli!

Anche i torvi, anche i tristi, anche i ladri
hanno negli occhi la dolcezza
di chi sa, di chi ha capito: squadre

ordinate di fiori nel caos dell'esistenza.
In realtà, io, sono il ragazzo, loro
gli adulti. Io, che per l'eccesso della mia presenza,

non ho mai varcato il confine tra l'amore
per la vita e la vita . . .
Io, cupo d'amore, e, intorno, il coro

dei lieti, cui la realtà è amica.
Sono migliaia. Non posso amarne uno.
Ognuno ha la sua nuova, la sua antica

is the right one, and that nothing will be lost.
Yes, they're humble. And what will later be
their mediocre way of fulfilling

themselves (their destiny is mediocrity)
is just now dawning
over unknown trees, in which nature's

only starting to germinate, in a stasis
of supreme purity and courage.
Yes, by now, they've been invaded

by the evil inherited from
. their fathers—my own dark race.
But in what do they place their hopes? What ray

of light strikes them, in those faces
where the hairline, forelocks,
waves have a more than

bodily grace? . . . Sweetly rebellious
and yet content with the future of their fathers:
that's what makes them so beautiful!

The eyes of even the surly, thievish,
sad, have the knowing sweetness
of those who've understood: orderly

squads of flowers in the chaos of existence.
In reality I'm the boy, they're
the adults. I who by the excess of my presence

have never crossed the border between love
for life and life . . .
I gloomy with love, and all around me, the chorus

of the happy, for whom reality's a friend.
Thousands of them. It's impossible to love only one of them.
Each has his own new or ancient

bellezza, ch'è di tutti: bruno
o biondo, lieve o pesante, è il mondo
che io amo in lui—ed accomuno,

in lui—visione d'amore infecondo
e purissimo—le generazioni,
il corpo, il sesso. Affondo

ogni volta—nelle dolci espansioni,
nei fiati di ginepro—nella storia,
che è sempre viva, in ogni

giorno, ogni millennio. Il mio amore
è solo per la donna: infante e madre.
Solo per essa, impegno tutto il cuore.

Per loro, i miei coetanei, i figli, in squadre
meravigliose sparsi per pianure
e colli, per vicoli e piazzali, arde

in me solo la carne. Eppure, a volte,
mi sembra che nulla abbia la stupenda
purezza di questo sentimento. Meglio la morte

che rinunciarvi! Io devo difendere
questa enormità di disperata tenerezza
che, pari al mondo, ho avuto nascendo.

Forse nessuno è vissuto a tanta altezza
di desiderio—ansia funeraria
che mi riempie come il mare la sua brezza.

I pendii, i colli, l'erba millenaria,
le frane di fiori o di rifiuti, i rami secchi
o lucidi di guazza, l'aria

delle stagioni con i loro muretti
vecchi o recenti al sole . . . tutto questo
nasconde me e (ridete!) gli amici giovinetti

beauty, which all share: dark,
blond, slender, brawny, it is
the world I love in him; and within him—

vision of sterile, purest love—
I fuse the generations,
the body, sex. Each time I sink

—in sweet expansions, in
juniper breezes—into history,
which is always living, in each

day, each millennium. My love
is only for the woman: child and mother.
Only to her do I pledge all my heart.

As for my coevals, the sons in tribes
scattering wondrously over plains,
hills, in alleyways, squares, for them

only my flesh burns. Yet at times
I think nothing else has the wonderful
purity of this feeling. Better death

than to renounce it! I must defend this
desperate awesome tenderness,
which, like the world, was mine at birth.

Perhaps no one's ever lived at such peaks
of desire—funereal anxiety which
fills me as the sea its breezes.

Slopes, hills, grass a thousand years old,
landslides of flowers or garbage, branches
dry or glistening with dew, the air

of the seasons, with their recent
and ancient sunlit walls . . . all this
hides me and my (you laugh!) young friends

in cui nessun atto è disonesto
perché è senza tragedia il loro desiderio:
perché il loro sesso è integro, fresco.

Non potrei, altrimenti. Solo se leggero,
dentro la norma, sano, il figlio
può farmi nascere il pensiero

scuro e abbacinante: così solo gli somiglio
nella verifica infinita di un segreto
ch'è nel suo grembo impuro come un giglio.

E mille volte questo atto è da ripetere:
perché, non ripeterlo, significa provare
la morte come un dolore frenetico,

che non ha pari nel mondo vitale . . .
Non lo nascondo, se nulla ho mai nascosto:
l'amore, non represso, che mi invade,

l'amore di mia madre, non dà posto
a ipocrisia e viltà! Né ho ragione
per essere diverso, non conosco

il vostro Dio, io sono ateo: prigione
solo del mio amore, per il resto libero,
in ogni mio giudizio, ogni mia passione.

Io sono un uomo libero! Candido cibo
della libertà è il pianto: ebbene piangerò.
È il prezzo del mio «libito far licito»,

certo: ma l'amore vale tutto ciò che ho.
Sesso, morte, passione politica,
sono i semplici oggetti cui io do

il mio cuore elegiaco . . . La mia vita
non possiede altro. Potrei domani,
nudo come un monaco, lasciare la partita

in whom no act is dishonest
because their desire is without tragedy
since their sex is whole and fresh.

I couldn't, otherwise. Only the wholesome
normal healthy son can kindle my
darkly dazzling thought; and in only one way

do I resemble him, in the infinite
reascertaining of the lilylike
secret of his impure groin.

And a thousand times this act has to be
repeated, because not to
means to feel death like a frenzied pain

unequaled in the living world . . .
I don't conceal it, I who've never concealed
anything: the unrepressed love that invades me,

love for my mother, has no room
for hypocrisy or cowardice! Nor am I right
because I'm different; I don't know

your God; I'm an atheist: prisoner
only of my love, but in all else I'm free,
in every judgment, every passion.

I am a free man! Freedom's
honest food is tears; well, then I'll weep.
It's the price of my legitimating my desire,

yes, but love's worth all I have.
Sex, death, political passion, these
are the simple objects to which I give

my elegiac heart . . . My life
possesses nothing else. I could, tomorrow,
naked as a monk, leave the worldly

mondana, cedere agli infami
la vittoria . . . Non avrebbe perso
nulla, certamente, la mia anima!

Ché la fatalità di essere esistenza
inalienabile, razza, universo,
basta a chiunque: anche se al mondo è senza

fraternità, perché diverso.
Perciò le risa e le allusioni
dei poveri razzisti, scorrono attraverso

la sua realtà come dei suoni
non reali, di morti. Nel mio essere,
questa realtà hanno sesso e passioni . . .

E, certo, non ne ho gioia. Ossesse
ne sono le sue predestinate forme:
«le repressioni fanno di me un Esse Esse,

o un mafioso . . .» e io—è enorme,
lo so—lo sono: giovane figlio candido
santo barbaro angelo, le orme

calcai, per qualche tempo, che mandano
alla Rivolta Reazionaria
(fu in epoche infime del grande

itinerario di una vita in Italia),
carnefice biondo, o killer colore
del fango, come un seguace . . . del sanguinario

borghese Hitler, o del forte figliolo
di poveri Giuliano . . .—conformismo
che mi salvava, come un volo

cieco. Tutto ciò non fu che crisma,
ombra che disparve dalla mia vita.
Rimase l'inclinazione allo scisma:

game, concede victory
to the infamous . . . Surely
my soul would lose nothing!—

because the fatal destiny of inalienable
existence, race, universe, is enough
for anyone, even if one is without brotherhood

in the world, because one is different.
And so the ridicule and insinuations
of pitiable racists run through

one's reality like unreal
sounds, of the dead. In my being,
sex and passions have this reality . . .

And it truly doesn't give me joy.
Its predestined forms are obsessive:
"repressions make me an S.S. man,

a Mafioso . . ." and this—it's terrible,
I know—is what I am: young innocent
saintly barbaric angelic son, for a time

I took the road leading to
Reactionary Revolt
(this was at the nadir of the grand

program of a life in Italy),
blond executioner or mud-colored killer,
like a disciple . . . of bloodthirsty

bourgeois Hitler or the strong son
of the poor, Salvatore Giuliano . . . conformity
that saved me, like a blind

escape. All this was only baptism,
a shadow which vanished from my life.
There remained the inclination toward schism,

un naturale bisogno di farmi male alla ferita
sempre aperta. Un configurare
ogni rapporto col mondo che a sé m'invita,

al rapporto del mio figliale
sadismo, masochismo: per cui non sono nato,
e sono qui solo come un animale

senza nome: da nulla consacrato,
non appartenente a nessuno,
libero d'una libertà che mi ha massacrato.

Onde non io, ma colui che comunico,
trae la disperata conclusione,
di essere il reietto di un raduno

di *altri: tutti gli uomini*, senza distinzione,
tutti i normali, di cui è questa vita.
E cerco alleanze che non hanno altra ragione

d'essere, come rivalsa, o contropartita,
che diversità, mitezza e impotente violenza:
gli Ebrei . . . i Negri . . . ogni umanità bandita . . .

E questa fu la via per cui da uomo senza
umanità, da inconscio succube, o spia,
o torbido cacciatore di benevolenza,

ebbi tentazione di santità. Fu la poesia.
La strega *buona* che caccia le streghe
per terrore, conobbe la democrazia . . .

Non fu un dono del cielo! Le atroci leghe
coi compagni virili inconsci ricattatori,
le risa con cui il mostro diede

dimostrazione di calma salute e sicuri amori,
pronto a torturare e uccidere altri mostri
pur di non essere riconosciuto—tutto fu fuori

a natural need to hurt myself at the always
open wound. A shaping of each
relationship-to-the-world-that-calls-me

into the form of my filial
sadism, masochism, to which I wasn't born,
and, here, I'm alone, like a nameless

animal, by nothing consecrated,
belonging to no one,
free with a freedom that's massacred me.

And so, not I but that man I communicate
must conclude, in despair, that
he's an outcast from the assembly

of *others: all men,* without distinctions,
all the normal, who constitute this life.
And I seek, as revenge or retaliation,

alliances that have no other reason for being
than otherness, meekness, powerless violence:
Jews . . . blacks . . . all outcast humanity . . .

And this was how, like a man without
humanity, an unwitting victim, or a spy
or confused seeker of others' goodwill,

I was tempted by holiness. Poetry was how.
The *good* witch—who, petrified with fear,
witch hunts—discovered democracy . . .

None of this came easily! The dreadful alliances
with virile comrades/unthinking blackmailers,
the laughter by which the monster

proved his calm health and secure loves,
ready to torture and kill other monsters
so as not to be recognized—all this was

d'improvviso da me (e vi si riconoscano
ora coloro che mi odiano, fatto pubblico,
i poveri fascisti), una sera, tra boschi

cedui, chissà, tra macchie indissolubili
di viole sulle prode, tra vigneti o lumi
serali di villaggi, sotto vergini nubi,

(nell'Emilia del mio destino, nel Friuli dei miei numi) . . .
A vincere fu il terrore. Voglio dire che fu
più grande il terrore della realtà e della solitudine,

di quello della società. Amara gioventù,
preda di quella immedicabile coscienza
di non esistere, che ancora è la mia schiavitù . . .

Ché io arriverò alla fine senza
aver fatto, nella mia vita
la prova essenziale, l'esperienza

che accomuna gli uomini, e dà loro
un'idea così dolcemente definita
di fraternità almeno negli atti dell'amore!

Come un cieco: a cui sarà sfuggita,
nella morte, una cosa che coincide
con la vita stessa,—luce seguita

senza speranza, e che a tutti sorride,
invece, come la cosa più semplice del mondo—
una cosa che non potrà mai condividere.

Morirò senza aver conosciuto il profondo
senso d'esser uomo, nato a una sola
vita, cui nulla, nell'eterno, corrisponde.

Un cieco, un mostro, in vita, non consola
mai niente davvero: ma al punto irrimediabile
e vergognoso, nel terrore dell'ora

suddenly out and away from me (here and now
may they recognize themselves, those who hate me,
exposed in public, pitiful fascists), one evening

in a young woods among indissoluble stains
of violets on the stream's edge, among vineyards
or the evening lights of the villages, under virgin clouds

(in the Emilia of my destiny, the Friuli of my deities) . . .
Terror won out. I mean, the terror of
reality and solitude was greater

than that of society. Bitter adolescence,
victim of that untreatable feeling
of nonbeing that still enslaves me . . .

For I'll arrive at the end of my
life without having passed
the essential test, the experience

that unites all men and gives them
their so-sweetly definite idea
of brotherhood, at least in the acts of love!

Like a blind man, to whom something that
coincides with life itself will have
escaped at death—light followed

hopelessly but which smiles on everyone,
like the simplest thing in the world—
something he'll never be able to share in.

Born into one single life that corresponds
to nothing in all eternity, I will die without
knowing the profound meaning of being a man.

A blind man, a monster, nothing in life can
ever really console him: but at the irremediable
shameful point, in the terror of the

in cui tutto è stato—egli sarà una cavia
neanche più un uomo! Assurdo
—da non poterlo sopportare, e gridare di rabbia,

e mugolare, come una bestia, il cui urlo
è l'urlo di un innocente che protesta
contro un'ingiustizia di cui è trastullo—

è questo ordine prenatale, questa
predestinazione, in cui egli non c'entra,
che nulla ha a che fare con la sua onesta

antica anima . . . Dentro i ventri
delle madri, nascono figli ciechi
—pieni di desiderio di luce—sbilenchi

—pieni d'istinti lieti:
e attraversano la vita nel buio e la vergogna.
Ci si può rassegnare—e i feti

viventi, povere erinni, possono in ogni
ora della loro vita, tacere o fingere.
Gli *altri* dicono sempre che non bisogna

essergli di peso. Ed essi obbediscono. Si tinge
così tutta la loro vita di un colore diverso.
E il mondo—il mondo innocente!—li respinge.

. . . .

Ma io parlo . . . del mondo—e dovrei,
invece—parlare dell'Italia, e anzi,
di *una* Italia, di quella di cui sei,

con me, lettore dei miei versi, figlio:
fisica storia in cui ti circostanzi.
L'ho chiamato «innocente», il mondo, io,

io, in quanto cieco, figlio martoriato.
Ma se guardo intorno questi avanzi
d'una storia che da secoli ha dato

ultimate hour—he'll be a ... guinea pig,
no longer even a man! Absurd
—to the point of being unendurable, screaming in rage,

howling like an animal whose cry
is the cry of an innocent protesting
an injustice of which he's the victim—

absurd this prenatal order, this
predestination in which he has no say
and which has nothing to do with his honest

ancient soul ... Within the mothers'
wombs, blind children are born—
longing for the light—misshapen—

full of joyous instincts:
and they go through life in darkness and shame.
One can be resigned to it—and the living

fetuses, wretched Erinyes, each moment
of their lives, know how to be silent and pretend.
The *others* always say they shouldn't

burden *them*. And they obey. And thus their whole
life assumes a wholly different color.
And the world—the innocent world!—rejects them.

. . . .

But I speak ... of the world—when instead
I should speak of Italy, or rather
an Italy, of which you, reader

of my poems, are, with me, the offspring:
that physical history in which you verify yourself.
I called it "innocent," the world, I,

I, the blind martyred son.
But if I look around me at these remnants
of a history that has for centuries produced

soltanto servi . . . questa Apparizione
in cui la realtà non ha altro indizio
che la sua brutale ripetizione . . .

che scena . . . espressionistica! Penso a un giudizio
subìto senza senso . . . le toghe . . . le tristi autorità del Sud . . .
dietro i visi dei giudici—in cui il vizio

è un vizio di dolore, che denuda
ambienti miserandi—non si leggeva che impotenza
a uscire da un'oscura realtà di parentele, da una cruda

moralità, da una provinciale inesperienza . . .
Quelle fronti da Teatro dell'Arte,
quei poveri occhi di obbedienti onagri

intestarditi, quelle orecchie basse,
quelle parole che per mascherare
il vuoto si gonfiavano a recitare una parte

di paterna minaccia, di indignazione floreale!
Ah, io non so odiare: e so quindi che non posso
descriverli con la ferocia necessaria

alla poesia. Dirò solo con pietà di quella faccia
di calabrese, con le forme del bambino
e del teschio, che parlava dialettale

con gli umili, scolastico coi grandi.
Che ascoltava attento, umano,
e intanto, negli ineffati e nefandi

fori interiori, covava il suo piano
di timido che il timore fa spietato.
Ai lati, altre due faccie ben riconoscibili,

faccie che per strada, in un bar affollato,
sono le faccie deboli, poco sane,
di precoci invecchiati, di malati

only serfs . . . this apparition
in which reality leaves no mark other
than its own brutal repetition . . .

what an . . . expressionistic scene! I think of a judgment
suffered pointlessly . . . the robes . . . sad Southern authorities . . .
behind the faces of the judges—whose faults

are the faults of those who've suffered
in poverty—one could see only the impossibility
of escaping an obscure reality of blood ties,

a crude morality, provincial inexperience . . .
Those Teatro dell'Arte foreheads,
those obedient, persistent onager's pitiable

eyes, those lowered ears,
those words that, to mask
the void, swell up to recite the role

of paternal menace and florid indignation!
Ah, I don't know how to hate: and so I know
I can't describe them with the ferocity necessary

to poetry. I'll speak only with pity of that
Calabrian face, with features both of
a child and a skull, who used dialect

with the humble, scholastic language with the grand . . .
who was listening carefully, humanely
and, meanwhile, within his unspoken, unspeakable

interior forums, was hatching his plan
of the timid whom fear makes ruthless.
At his side are two other easily recognizable faces,

faces from the street or a crowded bar,
weak, barely healthy faces of
the prematurely old, the jaundiced,

di fegato: di borghesi il cui pane
certo non sa di sale, non ignobili, no,
non prive affatto di sembianze umane

nel pungente nero degli occhi, nel pallore
delle fronti martoriate dalla prima
feroce anzianità . . . Un quarto inviato del Signore

—certo ammogliato, certo protetto da un giro
di rispettabili colleghi nella sua città
di provincia—rappreso in un sospiro

di malato nei visceri o nel cuore—
se ne stava in un banco isolato: come sta
chi si prepara a un premeditato disamore.

E davanti a questi, il campione: colui che ha
venduto l'anima al diavolo, in carne e ossa.
Classico personaggio! Avevo visto la sua faccia

alcuni mesi avanti: ed era un'altra:
la faccia di un giovanotto di grana grossa,
campagnola, stempiato e smunto

dalla dignità professionale.
Ora una vampa lo deformava:
come una vecchia crosta rossa

sopra la pelle. La luce prava
degli occhi era quella di chi è in colpa.
Il suo odio per la mia persona era l'odio

per l'oggetto di quella colpa, ossia
l'odio verso la sua coscienza.
Non era abbastanza disonesto. La fantasia

non basta a immaginare un'esperienza
di ignoranza e ricatto. La borghesia
è il diavolo: vendergli l'anima senza

the bourgeois from whom no salt tears pour,
though not at all ignoble, no,
not at all lacking human features,

in the pungent black of their eyes, in the pallor
of foreheads tortured by the first
ferocious signs of aging . . . A fourth envoy of the Lord

—married, surely; surely protected by a circle
of respectable colleagues in his provincial
town—curdled in the sigh of someone

with a bad stomach or weak heart—was sitting
alone on an isolated bench, as though preparing
for a premeditated estrangement.

And in front of these, the champion: who sold
himself body and soul to the devil.
Classic character! I'd seen his face

some months earlier, and it had looked different:
the peasant face of a coarse young
man, balding, colorless,

but with a professional dignity.
Now a blush was deforming him,
like an old red scab

on his skin. The depraved light
in his eyes was that of the guilty.
His hate for what I stood for was hate

for the object of that guilt, that is,
hate for his conscience.
He wasn't dishonest enough. His imagination

wasn't big enough to conceive of an experience
of ignorance and blackmail. The bourgeoisie
is the devil; should one sell it one's soul

contropartita? Oh, certo no: bisogna
adottare la sua cultura, recitare
come un Pater Noster la vergogna

dell'esordio puramente formale,
della clausola mistificatrice . . .
Ed essere retorici significa odiare,

essere incolti significa aver perso
deliberatamente ogni rispetto per l'uomo,
Il vecchio amore per l'ideale si riduce

a fingere disperatamente con se stessi,
a credere in ciò che mentendo si dice.
Ma la luce dell'occhio rimane, ossessi

accusatori! Lì, in quella goccia di luce,
nello sguardo sfuggente, livido,
colpevole—era la vostra verità.

Al rapporto con voi mi conduce,
lo so, una mia interiore volontà:
ma questo è un segreto dell'io,

o Dio, come voi dite. A voi si dirà:
«Voi non contate, siete simboli
di milioni di uomini: d'una società.

Questa mi condanna, non voi, suoi automi.
Ebbene: sono felice della mia mostruosità.
O vogliamo ingannare lo spirito? Uomini

che condannano uomini in nome del nulla:
perché le Istituzioni sono nulla, quando
hanno perso ogni forza, la forza fanciulla

delle Rivoluzioni—perché nulla
è la Morale del buon senso, di una
comunità passiva, senza più realtà.

with no compensation? Certainly not;
one must adopt its culture, reciting
like a Pater Noster the shame

of a purely formal preface,
of a misleading clause . . .
And to be rhetorical means to hate,

to be uncultured means to have lost
deliberately all respect for man.
The old love for the ideal is reduced to

a desperate lying to oneself
and believing the lies.
But the light of the eye remains, obsessed

accusers! There, in that drop of light,
in that elusive glance, livid,
guilty, was your truth.

I know that some will inside me
summons me to you,
but that's a secret of the self,

or God, if you wish. To you it will be said:
"You don't count, you're the symbols
of millions of men, of a society.

And it—not you, its automatons—condemns me.
Well then, I'm content to be a monster.
Or shall we cheat the spirit? Men

condemning men in the name of nothing:
because Institutions are nothing when
they've lost all their force, the maiden force of

Revolutions—because the Morality
of common sense, of a passive community
with no remaining reality, is nothing.

Voi, uomini formali—umili
per viltà, ossequienti per timidezza—
siete persone: in voi e in me, si consumi

il rapporto: in voi, di arido odio,
in me, di conoscenza. Ma per la società
di cui siete inespressivi rapsodi,

ben altro io ho da dire: non da marxista
più, o ancora, ma, per un momento
—se il rapimento degli Autori

dell'Apocalisse affabula in un fuoco
che non ha tempo: I miei amori—
griderò—sono un'arma terribile:

perché non l'uso? Nulla è più terribile
della diversità. Esposta ogni momento
—gridata senza fine—eccezione

incessante—follia sfrenata
come un incendio—contraddizione
da cui ogni giustizia è sconsacrata.

Ah Negri, Ebrei, povere schiere
di segnati e diversi, nati da ventri
innocenti, a primavere

infeconde, di vermi, di serpenti,
orrendi a loro insaputa, condannati
a essere atrocemente miti, puerilmente violenti,

odiate! straziate il mondo degli uomini bennati!
Solo un mare di sangue può salvare,
il mondo, dai suoi borghesi sogni destinati

a farne un luogo sempre più irreale!
Solo una rivoluzione che fa strage
di questi morti, può sconsacrarne il male!»

You, men of form—humble because
mediocre, obsequious because afraid—
you are people: let us consummate, you and I,

our relationship—in you, of arid hate,
in me, of knowledge. But, about the society
of which you are inexpressive rhapsodists,

I have something quite different to say: not as a Marxist
anymore, or, perhaps yes but for this moment only
—since the rapture of the Authors

of the Apocalypse is mythified
in a timeless fire: My loves—
I'll shout—are a terrible weapon;

why don't I use it? Nothing's more terrible
than being different. Exposed every moment
—shouted ceaselessly—incessant

exception—madness unrestrained
like a fire—contradiction
by which all justice is desecrated.

Oh, blacks, Jews, poor hosts
of the marked and different, born from
innocent wombs into sterile

springtimes, of worms and serpents,
horrendous without their knowing, condemned
to be atrociously meek, childishly violent,

hate! tear apart the world of well-born men!
Only a bloodbath can save the world
from its bourgeois dreams, certain

to make it more and more unreal!
Only a revolution that slaughters
these dead men can deconsecrate their evil!"

Questo può urlare, un profeta che non ha
la forza di uccidere una mosca—la cui forza
è nella sua degradante diversità.

Solo detto questo, o urlato, la mia sorte
si potrà liberare: e cominciare
il mio discorso sopra la realtà.

    (1962)

This is what a prophet would shout who doesn't have
the strength to kill a fly—whose strength
lies in his degrading difference.

Only when this has been said, or shouted,
will my fate be able to free itself,
and begin my discourse on reality.

(1962)

I sogni del mattino: quando
il sole già regna,
in una maturità
che sa solo il venditore ambulante,
che da molte ore cammina per le strade
con una barba di malato
sulle grinze della sua povera gioventù:
quando il sole regna
su reami di verdure già calde, su tende
stanche, su folle
i cui panni sanno già oscuramente di miseria
—e già centinaia di tram sono andati e tornati
per le rotaie dei viali che circondano la città,
inesprimibilmente profumati,

i sogni delle dieci del mattino,
nel dormente, solo,
come un pellegrino nella sua cuccia,
uno sconosciuto cadavere
—appaiono in lucidi caratteri greci,
e, nella semplice sacralità di due tre sillabe,
piene, appunto, del biancore del sole trionfante—
diviano una realtà,
maturata nel profondo e ora già matura, come il sole,
a essere goduta, o a fare paura.

Cosa mi dice il sogna mattutino?
«il mare, con lente ondate, grandiose, di grani azzurri,
si abbatte, lavorando con furore uterino,
irriducibile,
e quasi felice—perché dà felicità
il verificare anche l'atto più atroce del destino—
sgretola la tua isola, che ormai
è ridotta a pochi metri di terra . . .»

Aiuto, avanza la solitudine!

The dreams of morning,
when the sun's already ruling,
in a ripening
only the peddler knows,
walking the streets for hours,
the beard of the sickly
on the furrows of his poor youth—
when the sun rules
realms of already hot produce, weary
awnings, crowds
whose clothes already faintly smell of poverty
—and by now hundreds of trams have commenced
and returned on the tracks of the inexpressibly perfumed
boulevards surrounding the city,

dreams of ten in the morning,
of the sleeper, alone
like a pilgrim on his pallet,
unidentified corpse
—dreams embodied by lucid Greek characters,
by the simple sacredness of two or three syllables,
as though full of the triumphant sun's whiteness—
foretelling a reality
matured in unseen depths and now ripe, like the sun,
to be enjoyed or feared.

What does the morning dream say to me?
"The sea, with grandly slow waves of blue grain,
plunges downward, working with uterine fury,
irreducible,
and almost happy—because there's happiness
in verifying even the worst of destiny's atrocities,
eroding your island, now
only a few feet of earth . . ."

Help . . . the solitude's advancing!

Non importa se so che l'ho voluta, come un re.

Nel sonno, in me, un bambino muto si spaventa,
e chiede pietà, si affanna a correre ai ripari,
con un'agitazione
che «la virtù dismaga», povera creatura.
Lo atterrisce l'idea
di essere solo
come un cadavere in fondo alla terra.

Addio, dignità, nel sogno, sia pur mattutino!
Chi deve piangere piange,
chi deve aggrapparsi alle falde delle vesti altrui,
si aggrappa, e le tira, e le tira,
perché si voltino quelle faccie colore del fango,
e lo guardino negli occhi terrorizzati
per informarsi della sua tragedia,
per capire quanto sia spaventoso il suo stato!

Il biancore del sole, su tutto,
come un fantasma che la storia
preme sulle palpebre
col peso dei marmi barocchi o romanici . . .

Ho voluto la mia solitudine.
Per un processo mostruoso
che forse potrebbe rivelare
solo un sogno fatto dentro un sogno . . .

E, intanto, sono solo.
Perduto nel passato.
(Perché l'uomo ha un periodo solo, nella sua vita.)

Di copo i miei amici poeti,
che condividono con me il brutto biancore
di questi Anni Sessanta,
uomini e donne, appena un po' più anziani
o più giovani—sono là, nel sole.

Non ho saputo avere la grazia
per tenermeli stretti—nell'ombra di una vita

No matter that, like a king, I willed it.

In my sleep, a child frightened silent
asks for pity, runs frantically for shelter
with an agitation
that conquers virtue, poor creature.
The idea terrifies him
of being alone
like a corpse deep in the earth.

Good-by, dignity, in my morning dream!
He who must weep weeps,
he who must grab at the hems of others' clothes
will, and pulls them, pulls them,
so that these mud-colored faces turn to
look into his terrorized eyes
to learn of his tragedy, to understand
how frightening it is to be who he is!

The sun's whiteness on everything
like a ghost that history
presses on the eyelids with
the heaviness of baroque or Romanesque statues . . .

I willed my solitude—
by a monstrous process
that could perhaps reveal
only a dream dreamed inside a dream . . .

And, meanwhile, I'm alone.
Lost in the past.
(For our lives have only that one period.)

Suddenly my poet friends,
who share with me the ugly whiteness
of these sixties,
men and women only slightly older
or younger—are there, in the sun.
I didn't have the grace
to cherish them—in the shade of a life

che si svolge troppo attaccata
all'accidia radicale della mia anima.

La vecchiaia, poi, ha fatto
di mia madre e di me
due maschere
che nulla hanno peraltro perduto
della tenerezza mattutina
—e l'antica rappresentazione
si ripete
nell'autenticità
che solo sognando dentro un sogno,
potrei forse chiamare col suo nome.

Tutto il mondo è il mio corpo insepolto.

Atollo sbriciolato
dalle percosse dei grani azzurri del mare.

Cosa fare, se non, nella veglia, avere dignità?
È giunta l'ora dell'esilio,
forse: l'ora in cui un antico avrebbe dato realtà
alla realtà,
e la solitudine maturata intorno a lui,
avrebbe avuto la forma della solitudine.

E io invece—come nel sogno—
mi accanisco a darmi illusioni, penose,
di lombrico paralizzato da forze incomprensibili:
«ma no! ma no! è solo un sogno!
la realtà
è fuori, nel sole trionfante,
nei viali e nei caffè vuoti,
nella suprema afonia della dieci del mattino,
un giorno come tutti gli altri, con la sua croce!»

Il mio amico dal mento di papa, il mio
amico dall'occhio marroncino . . .
i miei cari amici del Nord
fondati su affinità elettive dolci come la vita
—sono là, nel sole.

unfolding too attached to
my soul's essential sloth.

Age, then, made
of my mother and me
two masks
that have lost nothing, though,
of morning's tenderness
—and the ancient rite
recurs
in its authentic form,
which only by dreaming inside a dream
could I perhaps call by its true name.

All the world is my unburied body.

Atoll crumbled
by the blows of the sea's blue grains.

What else to do but in the vigil have dignity?
The hour of exile is here,
perhaps—when an ancient
could have given reality to reality,
and the solitude ripening around him
would have had the form of solitude.

And I instead—as in a dream—again
and again inflict on myself painful images,
of the earthworm paralyzed by incomprehensible forces:
"No! No! It's only a dream!
Reality's
outside, in the triumphant sun,
in the boulevards, in the empty cafés,
in the supreme aphonia of ten in the morning,
a day like any other with its cross!"

My friend with the pope's chin, my
friend with the light brown eyes . . .
my dear friends from the North
rooted in elective affinities sweet as life
—are there, in the sun.

Anche Elsa, col suo biondo dolore,
lei—destriero ferito, caduto,
sanguinante—è là.

E mia madre mi è vicina . . .
ma oltre ogni limite di tempo:
siamo due superstiti in uno.
I suoi sospiri, qua, nella cucina,
i suoi malori a ogni ombra di degradante notizia,
a ogni sospetto della ripresa
dell'odio del branco di goliardi che ghignano
sotto la mia stanza di agonizzante
—non sono che la naturalezza della mia solitudine.

Come una moglie messa nel rogo col re,
o sepolta con lui
in una tomba che se ne va come una barchetta
verso i millenni—la fede degli Anni Cinquanta,
è qui con me, già leggermente oltre i limiti del tempo,
a farsi sgretolare anch'essa
dalla pazienza furibonda dei grani azzurri del mare.

E . . .
i miei amori di pura sensualità,
replicati nelle valli sacre della libidine,
sadica, masochista, i calzoni
con la loro sacca tiepida
dove è segnato il destino di un uomo
—sono atti che io compio solo
in mezzo al mare stupendamente sconvolto.

Piano piano le migliaia di gesti sacri,
la mano sul gonfiore tiepido,
i baci, ogni volta a una bocca diversa,
sempre più vergine,
sempre più vicina all'incanto della specie,
alla norma che fa dei figli teneri padri,
piano piano
sono divenuti monumenti di pietra
che a migliaia affollano la mia solitudine.

Elsa, with her blond grief
—wounded, fallen, bleeding
steed—is also there.

And my mother's near me . . .
but past all limits of time:
we're two survivors in one.
Her sighs, here, in the kitchen,
her spells of faintness at each new hint of scandal,
at each suspicion of a resumption
of the hate of the herd of university boys smirking
below my room of a dying man's agonies
—these constitute the nature of my solitude.

Like a wife cast onto the pyre with the king
or buried alive with him
in a tomb that moves off like a skiff
toward the millennia—the faith of the 1950s
is here with me, already slightly past time's limits,
and it too will be crumbled
by the furious patience of the sea's blue grains.

And . . .
my loves of pure sensuality
repeated over and over in the sacred valleys of lust,
sadistic, masochistic, the trousers
with their warm sack
where a man's destiny is marked
—are acts I perform, alone,
in the midst of a wondrously convulsive sea.

Bit by bit the thousands of sacred gestures,
the hand on the warm swelling,
the kisses, each time to a different mouth,
always more virgin,
always nearer the enchantment of the species,
the norm that makes tender fathers of sons,
bit by bit
they've become stone monuments
which by the thousands crowd my solitude.

Attendono
che una nuova ondata di razionalità,
o un sogno fatto nel fondo di un sogno, ne parli.
Così mi desto,
ancora una volta:
e mi vesto, mi metto al tavolo di lavoro.
La luce del sole è già più matura,
i venditori ambulanti più lontani,
più acre, nei mercati del mondo, il tepore della verdura,
lungo viali dall'inesprimibile profumo,
sulle sponde di mari, ai piedi di vulcani.
Tutto il mondo è al lavoro, nella sua epoca futura.

Ah, belle bandiere degli Anni Quaranta!
Pretesto al buffone per piangere.

    (1962)

They're waiting
for a new wave of reason,
or a dream dreamed in the depths of a dream, to speak of them.
And so I wake
once again
and dress and sit down at the work table.
The sunlight has ripened further,
the peddlers are farther away,
the warm produce is more acrid, in the markets of the world,
along inexpressibly perfumed boulevards,
on shores of seas, at the foot of volcanoes.
The whole world is at work, in its future epoch.

Ah, beautiful banners of the 1940s!
Pretext for the clown to cry.

   (1962)

UNA DISPERATA VITALITÀ

I

(Stesura, in «cursus» di linguaggio «gergale»
corrente, dell'antefatto: Fiumicino, il vecchio
castello e una prima idea vera della morte.)

Come in un film di Godard: solo
in una macchina che corre per le autostrade
del Neo-capitalismo latino—di ritorno dall'aeroporto—
[là è rimasto Moravia, puro fra le sue valige]
    solo, «pilotando la sua Alfa Romeo»
         in un sole irriferibile in rime
         non elegiache, perché celestiale
         —il più bel sole dell'anno—
come in un film di Godard:
         sotto quel sole che si svenava immobile
         unico,
    il canale del porto di Fiumicino
        —una barca a motore che rientrava inosservata
        —i marinai napoletani coperti di cenci di lana
        —un incidente stradale, con poca folla intorno . . .

—come in un film di Godard—riscoperta
del romanticismo in sede
di neocapitalistico cinismo, e crudeltà—
al volante
per la strada di Fiumicino,

ed ecco il castello (che dolce
mistero, per lo sceneggiatore francese,
nel turbato sole senza fine, secolare,

questo bestione papalino, coi suoi merli,
sulle siepi e i filari della brutta campagna
dei contadini servi) . . .

I

*(Draft, in progress, in current slang, of
what's gone before: Fiumicino, the old
castle, and a first true idea of death.)*

As in a film by Godard: alone
in a car moving along the highways
of Latin neocapitalism—returning from the airport—
[where Moravia remained, pure among his luggage]
      alone, "piloting his Alfa Romeo,"
          in a sun inexpressible in rhymes
          that aren't elegiac, because it's celestial
          —the most beautiful sun of the year—
as in a film by Godard:
          under that sole still sun slitting
          its veins,
     the canal of the port of Fiumicino
     —a motorboat returning unobserved
     —Neapolitan sailors in their wool rags
     —an auto accident, with a little crowd around it . . .

—as in a film by Godard—rediscovery
of romanticism in the seat of
neocapitalistic cynicism and cruelty—
at the wheel
on the road from Fiumicino,

and there's the castle (what sweet
mystery for the French screenwriter
in the troubled, endless, centuries-old sun,

this papal monster, with its crenelations
above the hedges and vine rows of the ugly
countryside of peasant serfs) . . .

—sono come un gatto bruciato vivo,
pestato dal copertone di un autotreno,
impiccato da ragazzi a un fico,

ma ancora almeno con sei
delle sue sette vite,
come un serpe ridotto a poltiglia di sangue
un'anguilla mezza mangiata

—le guance cave sotto gli occhi abbattuti,
i capelli orrendamente diradati sul cranio
le braccia dimagrite come quelle di un bambino
—un gatto che non crepa, Belmondo
che «al volante della sua Alfa Romeo»
nella logica del montaggio narcisistico
si stacca dal tempo, e v'inserisce
Se stesso:
in immagini che nulla hanno a che fare
con la noia delle ore in fila . . .
col lento risplendere a morte del pomeriggio . . .

La morte non è
nel non poter comunicare
ma nel non poter più essere compresi.

E questo bestione papalino, non privo
di grazia—il ricordo
delle rustiche concessioni padronali,
innocenti, in fondo, com'erano innocenti
le rassegnazioni dei servi—
nel sole che fu,
nei secoli,
per migliaia di meriggi,
qui, il solo ospite,

questo bestione papalino, merlato
accucciato tra pioppeti di maremma,
campi di cocomeri, argini,
questo bestione papalino blindato
da contrafforti del dolce color arancio
di Roma, screpolati

—I'm like a cat burned alive,
crushed by a truck's tires,
hanged by boys to a fig tree,

but still with at least eight
of its nine lives, like
a snake reduced to a bloody pulp,
an eel half-eaten

—sunken cheeks under dejected eyes,
hair horribly thinned on skull,
arms skinny as a child's,
—a cat that doesn't die, Belmondo
who "at the wheel of his Alfa Romeo"
within the logic of the narcissistic montage
detaches himself from time, and inserts in it
himself,
in images that have nothing to do with
the boredom of the hours in a line,
the slow splendid death of the afternoon . . .

Death is not
in not being able to communicate
but in no longer being able to be understood.

And this papal monster, not devoid
of grace—reminder of
the rustic condescensions of patronage,
which were innocent, in the end, as the serfs'
submissiveness was innocent—
in the sun that was,
through the centuries,
for thousands of afternoons,
here, the only guest,

this papal monster, crenelated,
crouched among poplar groves and marshes,
fields of watermelons, embankments,
this papal monster, armored
by buttresses the sweet orange color
of Rome, cracking

come costruzioni di etruschi o romani,
sta per non poter più essere compreso.

11

(Senza dissolvenza, a stacco netto, mi rappresento
in un atto—privo di precedenti storici—di
«industria culturale».)

Io volontariamente martirizzato . . . e,
lei di fronte, sul divano:
campo e controcampo, a rapidi flash,
«Lei—so che pensa, guardandomi,
in più domestica-italica M.F.
sempre alla Godard—lei, specie di Tennessee!»,
il cobra col golfino di lana
            (col cobra subordinato
            che screma in silenzio magnesio).
Poi forte: «Mi dice che cosa sta scrivendo?»

«Versi, versi, scrivo! versi!
(maledetta cretina,
versi che lei non capisce priva com'è
di cognizioni metriche! Versi!)
VERSI NON PIÙ IN TERZINE!

            Capisce?
Questo è quello che importa: non più in terzine!
Sono tornato tout court al magma!
Il Neo-capitalismo ha vinto, sono
sul marciapiede
            come poeta, ah [singhiozzo]
            e come cittadino [altro singhiozzo].»
E il cobro con il biro:
«Il titolo della Sua opera?» «Non so . . .
[Egli parla ora sommesso come intimidito, rivestendo
la parte che il colloquio, accettato, gli impone di
fare: come sta poco
a stingere
la sua grinta
in un muso di mammarolo condannato a morte]

like Etruscan or Roman buildings,
is at the point of no longer being understood.

    11

(Without a dissolve, in a sharp cut, I portray myself
in an act—without historical precedents—of "cultural
industry.")

I, voluntarily martyred . . . and
she in front of me, on the couch:
shot and countershot in rapid flashes,
"You"—I know what she's thinking, looking at me,
in a more domestic-Italian *Masculine-Feminine,*
always à la Godard—"you, sort of a Tennessee!"
the cobra in the light wool sweater
        (and the subordinate cobra
        gliding in magnesium silence).
Then aloud: "Tell me what you're writing?"

"Poems, poems, I'm writing! Poems!
(stupid idiot,
poems she wouldn't understand, lacking as she is
in metric knowledge! Poems!)
poems NO LONGER IN TERCETS!

      Do you understand?
This is what's important: no longer in tercets!
I have gone back, plain and simple, to the magma!
Neocapitalism won, I've
been kicked out on the street
      as a poet [boo-hoo]
      and citizen [another boo-hoo]."
And the cobra with the ballpoint:
"The title of your work?" "I don't know . . .
[He speaks softly now, as though intimidated, assuming
the role the interview, once accepted, imposes
on him: how little it takes
for his sinister mug
to fade into
the face of a mama's boy condemned to death]

—forse... ‹La Persecuzione›
    o... ‹Una nuova preistoria› (o Preistoria)
    o...
[E qui si inalbera, riacquista
la dignità dell'odio civile]
    ‹Monologo sugli Ebrei› ...
        [Casca
il discorso come la debolezza dell'arsi
dell'ottonario scombinato: magmatico!]
«E di che parla?»
«Beh, della mia... della Sua, morte.
Non è nel non comunicare, [la morte]
ma nel non essere compresi...

        (Se lo sapesse, il cobra
        ch'è una fiacca pensata
        fatta tornando da Fiumicino!)
Sono quasi tutte liriche, la cui composizione
di tempo e luogo
consiste, strano!, in una corsa in automobile...
meditazioni dai sessanta ai centoventi all'ora...
con veloci panoramiche, e carrellate
a seguire o a precedere
su significativi monumenti, o gruppi
di persone, spronanti
a un oggettivo amore... di cittadino
(o utente della strada)...»

«Ah, ah—[è la cobra con la biro che ride]—e...
chi è che *non comprende*?»
«Coloro che non ci appartengono più.»

    III

Coloro che non ci appartengono più!
Trascinati da un nuovo soffio della storia
ad altre vite, con le loro innocenti gioventù!

Ricordo che fu... per un amore
che m'invadeva gli occhi castani e gli onesti calzoni
la casa e la campagna, il sole del mattino e il sole

—perhaps . . . 'The Persecution'
    or . . . 'A New Prehistory' (or Prehistory)
    or . . .
[And here he rears up, regaining
the dignity of civil hate]
    'Monologue on the Jews' . . ."
                          [The discourse
flounders like the weak unaccented beat
of a jumbled octosyllable: magmatic!]
"And what's it about?"
"Well, my . . . your, death.
It is not in not communicating [death],
but in not being understood . . .

        (If she only knew, the cobra,
           that this is a tired idea
           concocted coming back from Fiumicino!)
They're almost all lyrics, whose composition
in time and space
consists (strangely enough!) of an automobile ride . . .
meditations from forty to eighty miles per hour . . .
with quick pans (and dollies
following or preceding them),
over significant monuments, or groups
of people, inducing
an objective love . . . by the citizen
(or user of the road) . . ."

"Ha, ha—[it's the cobress with the ballpoint, laughing] and . . .
who is it that *doesn't understand*?"
"Those no longer among us."

   III

Those no longer among us!
Lifted, with their innocent youth,
by a new breath of history, to other lives!

I remember it was . . . because of a love
that invaded my brown eyes and honest trousers,
the house and countryside, morning sun

della sera . . . nei sabati buoni
del Friuli, nelle . . . Domeniche . . . Ah!, non posso
neanche pronunciare questa parola della passioni

vergini, della mia morte (vista in un fosso
secco formicolante di primule,
tra filari tramortiti dall'oro, a ridosso

di casolari scuri contro un azzurro sublime).

Ricordo che in quell'amore mostruoso
giungevo a gridare di dolore
per le domeniche quando dovrà splendere

«sopra i figli dei figli, il sole!»

Piangevo, nel lettuccio di Casarsa,
nella camera che sapeva di orina e bucato
in quelle domeniche che splendevano a morte . . .

Lacrime incredibili! Non solo
per quello che perdevo, in quel momento
di struggente immobilità dello splendore,

ma per quello che avrei perso! Quando
nuove gioventù—che non potevo neanche pensare,
così uguali a quelle che ora si vestivano

di calzettoni bianchi e di giubbetti inglesi,
col fiore all'occhiello—o di stoffe
scure, per nozze, trattate con figliale gentilezza,

—avrebbero popolato la Casarsa delle vite future,
immutata, coi suoi sassi, e il suo sole
che la copriva di moribonda acqua d'oro . . .

Per un impeto epilettico di dolore
omicida, protestavo
come un condannato all'ergastolo, chiudendomi
in camera,

and evening sun . . . on the good Saturdays
of Friuli, on the . . . Sundays . . . Ah, I can't
even utter that word of virgin

passions, of my death (seen in a dry
ditch swarming with primroses, between
vine rows stunned by gold, next to

dark farmhouses against a sublime blue sky).

I remember that in that monstrous love
I nearly screamed in pain
for the Sundays when the sun must shine

"above the sons of the sons!"

I was crying, in my narrow bed, in Casarsa,
in the room that smelled of urine and laundry
on those Sundays with their dying glow . . .

Incredible tears! Not only
for what I was losing, in that moment
of heartrending immobility of splendor,

but for what I would lose! When new
young men—of whom I couldn't conceive,
so like those dressing now

in heavy white trousers and tight English jackets,
with a flower in the buttonhole, or in dark
cloth, for weddings, cared for with filial kindness

—would populate the Casarsa of future lives,
unchanged, with its stones, and its sunlight
covering it in golden water . . .

Through an epileptic impulse of homicidal
grief, I was protesting
like someone sentenced to life imprisonment, locking myself
in my room,

senza che del resto nessuno lo sapesse,
a urlare, con la bocca
tappata dalle coperte annerite
per le bruciature del ferro da stiro,
le care coperte di famiglia,
su cui covavo i fiori della mia gioventù.

E un dopopranza, o una sera, urlando
sono corso,
per le strade della domenica, dopo la partita,
al cimitero vecchio, là dietro la ferrovia,
e compiere, e a ripetere, fino al sangue,
l'atto più dolce della vita,
io solo, sopra il mucchietto di terra
di due o tre tombe
di soldati italiani o tedeschi
senza nome sulle croci di assi
—sepolti lì dal tempo dell'altra guerra.

E la notte, poi, tra le secche lacrime i corpi
sanguinanti di quei poveri ignoti
vestiti di panni grigioverdi

vennero in grappolo sopra il mio letto
dove dormivo nudo e svuotato,
a sporcarmi di sangue, fino all'aurora.

Avevo vent'anni, neanche—diciotto,
diciannove . . . ed era già passato un secolo
dacché ero vivo, una intera vita

consumata al dolore dell'idea
che non avrei mai potuto dare il mio amore
se non alla mia mano, o all'erba dei fossi,

o magari al terriccio di una tomba incustodita . . .
Vent'anni, e, con la sua storia umana, e il suo ciclo
di poesia, era conclusa una vita.

without anybody else knowing,
to scream, mouth stuffed with
the blankets darkened by
the burns of the irons,
the dear blankets of the family,
on which I was brooding over the flowers of my youth.

And one afternoon, or one evening, I ran,
screaming,
through the streets of Sunday, after the game,
to the old cemetery, there, beyond the railroad tracks,
and performed, and repeated, till I bled,
the sweetest act of life,
I alone, on the little pile of earth,
the graves of two or three
Italian or German soldiers,
no names on the wood-plank crosses
—buried there since the other war.

And that night, amid my dry tears, the bleeding
bodies of those poor unknowns
dressed in olive drab

appeared in a cluster above my bed
where I was sleeping, naked and emptied,
to smear me with blood till the sun rose.

I was twenty, no, less—eighteen,
nineteen . . . and a century had already passed
since my birth, an entire lifetime

consumed in the pain of the idea
that I would never be able to give my love
except to my hand, or the grassy ditches,

or perhaps the earth of an unguarded grave . . .
Twenty years, and, with its human history, and its cycle
of poetry, a life had ended.

*(Ripresa dell'intervista, e confuse spiegazioni
sulla funzione del marxismo, ecc.)*

(Ah, non è che una visita al mondo, la mia!)

Ma ritorniamo alla realtà.

[Lei è qui, con la faccia visibilmente preoccupata ma alleggerita
dalla buona educazione, che aspetta, nell'inquadratura «grigia»,
secondo la buona regola del classicismo francese. Un Léger.]

«Secondo lei allora—fa, reticente,
mordicchiando il biro—qual'è
la funzione del marxista?» E si accinge a notare.

«Con . . . delicatezza da batteriologo . . . direi [balbetto,
        preso da impeti di morte]
spostare masse da eserciti napoleonici, staliniani . . .
        con miliardi di annessi . . .
        in modo che . . .
        la massa che si dice conservatrice
        [del Passato] lo perda:
        la massa rivoluzionaria, lo acquisti
        riedificandolo nell'atto di vincerlo . . .
        È per l'Istinto di Conservazione
        che sono comunista!
                Uno spostamento
da cui dipende vita e morte: nei secoli dei secoli.

        Farlo pian piano, come quando
                un capitano del genio svita
                la sicura di una bomba inesplosa, e,
per un attimo, può restare al mondo
(coi suoi moderni caseggiati, intorno, al sole)
                o esserne cancellato per sempre:

                una sproporzione inconcepibile
                tra i due corni!

IV

*(Resumption of the interview, and confused explanations
of the function of Marxism, etc.)*

(Mine is only a visit to the world!)

But, to return to reality.

[She's here, her face visibly worried, but softened by
good manners, waiting in a "grey" shot, in accordance with
the good rules of French classicism. A Léger.]

"According to you then"—she says reticently,
nibbling her ballpoint—"what's
the function of the Marxist?" And she gets ready to take notes.

"With . . . the delicacy of the bacteriologist . . . I'd say [I stammer,
        seized by impulses of death]
to move masses like Napoleonic, Stalinist armies . . .
        with billions of annexings . . .
        so that . . .
        the masses that call themselves conservative [of
        the past] lose it, while
        the revolutionary masses acquire it,
        rebuilding it in the act of defeating it . . .
        It is because of the instinct of conservation
        that I'm a communist!
                A move
on which depend life and death through the centuries forever and ever.

        To do it slowly, as when
                an army engineer unscrews
                the safety catch of an unexploded bomb, and,
        for a moment, can remain in the world
        (with its modern city blocks, all around him, in the sunlight)
                or be erased from it forever:

                an inconceivable distance
                between the two horns!

Uno spostamento
da fare piano piano, tirando il collo,
chinandosi, raggricciandosi sul ventre,
mordendosi le labbra o stringendo gli occhi
come un giocatore di bocce
che, dimenandosi, cerca di dominare
il corso del suo tiro, di rettificarlo
verso una soluzione
che imposterà la vita nei secoli.»

v

La vita nei secoli...
A questo alludeva
dunque—ieri sera...
rattrappito nel breve segmento del suo gemito—
quel treno lontano...

Quel treno che gemeva
sconsolato, come stupito di esistere,
(e, insieme, rassegnato—perché ogni atto
della vita è un segmento già segnato in una linea
che è la vita stessa, chiara solo nel sogno)

gemeva quel treno, e l'atto del gemere
—impensabilmente lontano, oltre le Appie
e i Centocelle del mondo—
si univa a un altro atto: unione casuale,
mostruosa, cervellotica
e tanto privata
che solo oltre la linea dei miei occhi
magari chiusi, è possibile averne conoscenza...

Atto d'amore, il mio. Ma perso nella miseria
di un corpo concesso per miracolo,
nella fatica del nascondersi, nell'ansare
lungo una cupa strada ferrata, nel pestare il fango
in una campagna coltivata da giganti...

La vita nei secoli...
come una stella cadente

A move
to be made bit by bit, stretching the neck,
stooping, tightening the belly,
biting one's lips or squinting
like a bocce player
who, twisting his body, seeks to dominate
the course of his throw, to rectify it
toward a solution
that will map out life through the centuries."

v

Life through the centuries . . .
This then is what was being
hinted at—last evening . . .
stunned in the brief segment of its wailing—
by that distant train . . .

That train that was wailing,
disconsolate, as though astonished to exist
(and, at the same time, resigned—because every act
of life is a segment already marked in a line
that is life itself, clear only in dreams)

that train was wailing, and the act of wailing
—unthinkably distant, beyond the Appian Ways
and Centocelles of the world—
was joining another act: chance union,
monstrous, bizarre
and so private
that only behind the line of my eyes,
which were perhaps closed, is it possible to know of it . . .

This is my act of love, but lost in the misery
of a body vouchsafed by miracle,
lost in the stress of hiding, in gasping
alongside a gloomy railroad track, in stalking
a muddy countryside farmed by giants . . .

Life through the centuries . . .
like a star falling

oltre il cielo dei giganteschi ruderi,
oltre le proprietà dei Caetani o dei Torlonia,
oltre le Tuscolane e le Capannelle del mondo—
quel gemito meccanico diceva:
la vita nei secoli . . .

E i miei sensi erano lì ad ascoltarlo.

Accarezzavo una testa arruffata e polverosa,
del color biondo che bisogna avere nella vita,
del disegno che vuole il destino,
e un corpo di cavallino agile e tenero
con la ruvida tela dei vestiti che sanno di madre:
compivo un atto d'amore,
ma i miei sensi stavano ad ascoltare:

la vita nei secoli . . .

Poi la testa bionda del destino disparve
da un pertugio,
nel pertugio fu il cielo bianco della notte,
finché, contro quel lembo di cielo, apparve
un'altra pettinatura, un'altra nuca;
nera, forse, o castana: e io
nella grotta perduta nel cuore dei possessi
dei Caetani o i Torlonia
tra i ruderi costruiti da giganti seicenteschi
in giorni immensi di carnevale, io
ero coi sensi ad ascoltare . . .

la vita nei secoli . . .

Più volte nel pertugio contro il biancore
della notte che si perdeva
oltre le Casiline del mondo,
sparì e riapparve la testa del destino,
con la dolcezza ora della madre meridionale
ora del padre alcolizzato, sempre la stessa
testolina arruffata e polverosa, o già

beyond the sky of gigantic ruins,
beyond the properties of the Caetanis or Torlonias,
beyond the Tuscolanas and Capannellas of the world—
this mechanical wail was saying:
life through the centuries . . .

And my senses were there to listen to it.

I was stroking a disheveled dusty head,
with the blond color it must have in life,
in the shape that destiny decrees,
the agile tender body of a colt, the rough cloth
of garments that have known a mother's care:
I was performing an act of love,
but my senses were there, listening:

life through the centuries . . .

Then the blond head of destiny disappeared
through a hole,
and the hole filled with the white sky of night,
until against the strip of sky appeared
another head of hair, another nape,
black, perhaps, or brown; and I,
in a grotto lost in the heart of the estates
of the Caetanis or Torlonias
among ruins built by seventeenth-century giants
in the immense days of the carnival, I
was there with my senses to listen . . .

life through the centuries . . .

Over and over in the hole,
as the pale night dispersed
beyond the Casilinas of the world,
disappeared and reappeared the head of destiny,
with the sweetness now of the southern mother,
now of the alcoholic father, always the same
dear little head, disheveled and dusty or already

composta nella vanità di una giovinezza popolare:
e io,
ero coi sensi ad ascoltare

la voce di un altro amore
—la vita nei secoli—
che si alzava purissima nel cielo.

V I

(Una vittoria fascista)

Mi guarda con pena.
«E . . . allora lei . . .—[sorriso mondano, goloso,
con coscienza della golosità e cattivante
ostentazione—occhi e denti fiammanti—
di un leggero titubante disprezzo infantile
verso di sé]—allora lei, è molto infelice!»

«Eh (devo ammetterlo)
sono in uno stato di confusione, signorina.

Rileggendo il mio libro dattiloscritto
di poesia (questo, di cui parliamo)
ho avuto la visione . . . oh, magari fosse
solo di un caos di contraddizioni—le rassicuranti
contraddizioni . . . No, è la visione
di un'anima confusa . . .

Ogni falso sentimento
produce la sicurezza assoluta di averlo.
Il mio falso sentimento era quello . . .
della salute. Strano! dicendolo a lei
—incomprensiva per definizione,
con quel viso di bambola senza labbra—
verifico ora con chiarezza clinica
il fatto
di non aver mai avuto, io, alcuna chiarezza.

combed up by the vanity of a working-class youth:
and I,
I was there with my senses to listen

to the voice of another love
—life through the centuries—
which was rising most pure into the sky.

    V I

(A fascist victory)

She looks at me pityingly
"And . . . but, then you—[worldly smile, greedy,
conscious of its greed and its captivating
ostentation—eyes and teeth sparkling
and with a slight hesitating infantile contempt
toward herself]—then you, you're very unhappy!"

"Ah (I must admit)
I'm in a state of confusion, signorina.

Rereading my typewritten book
of poems (this one that we're talking about)
I had the vision . . . oh, I wish it were
only of a chaos of contradictions—the reassuring
contradictions . . . No, it's the vision
of a confused soul . . .

Each false feeling
produces the absolute security of having it.
My false feeling was that . . .
of health. Strange! saying it to you
—uncomprehending by definition
with that lipless doll's face—
I verify now with clinical lucidity
the fact
of never having had any lucidity.

È vero che alle volte può bastare,
per essere sani (e chiari)
credere di esserlo . . . Tuttavia
(scriva, scriva!) la mia confusione
attuale è la conseguenza
di una vittoria fascista.

        [nuovi, incontrollati, fedeli
          impeti di morte]

Una piccola, secondaria vittoria.
Facile, poi. Io ero solo:
con le mie ossa, una timida madre
spaventata, e la mia volontà.

L'obbiettivo era umiliare un umiliato.
Devo dirle che ci sono riusciti,
e senza neanche molta fatica. Forse
se avessero saputo che era così semplice
si sarebbero scomodati di meno, e in meno!

(Ahi, parlo, vede, con un plurale generico: Essi!
con l'amore ammiccante del matto verso il proprio male.)

I risultati di questa vittoria, poi,
anch'essi, contano ben poco: una firma
autorevole in meno negli appelli di pace.
Beh, *a parte objecti,* non è molto.
A parte subjecti . . . Ma lasciamo stare:
ho descritto fin troppo,
e mai oralmente,
i miei dolori di verme pestato
che erige la sua testina e si dibatte
con ingenuità ripugnante, ecc.

Una vittoria fascista!
Scriva, scriva: sappiano (*essi!*) che lo so:

con la coscienza di un uccello ferito
che mitemente morendo non perdona.»

It's true that at times it's enough,
in order to be healthy (and lucid),
to believe that one is . . . Nevertheless
(keep on writing!) my present
confusion is the consequence
of a fascist victory.

> [new, uncontrolled, faithful
> impulses of death]

A small, secondary victory.
Easy, even. I was alone:
with my bones, a shy frightened
mother, and my will.

The objective was to humiliate the already humiliated.
I must tell you they've succeeded,
and without even much effort. Perhaps
if they'd known it was so simple,
they, and fewer of them, would have taken less trouble!

(Aha, notice, I'm using a generic plural: They!
with the winking love of the madman toward his illness.)

The results of this victory, then,
even they, count for very little: one authoritative
signature fewer on the petitions for peace.
Well, from the object's viewpoint, it's not much.
As for the subject . . . But let's leave it at that;
I've described too much even,
but never orally,
my sorrows of a crushed worm
who raises its little head and struggles,
with repugnant ingenuousness, etc.

A fascist victory!
Keep writing: let them *(them!)* know that I know:

with the consciousness of a wounded bird
that meekly dying doesn't forgive."

Non perdona!

C'era un'anima, tra quelle che ancora
dovevano scendere nella vita
—tante, e tutte uguali povere anime—
un'anima, in cui nella luce degli occhi castani,
nel modesto ciuffo pettinato da un'idea materna
della bellezza maschile,
ardeva il desiderio di morire.

La vide subito, colui
che non perdona.

La prese, la chiamò vicino a sé,
e, come un artigiano,
lassù nei mondi che precedono la vita,
le impose le mani sul capo
e pronunciò la maledizione.

Era un'anima candida e pulita,
come un ragazzetto alla prima comunione,
saggio della saggezza dei suoi dieci anni,
vestito di bianco, di una stoffa
scelta dall'idea materna della grazia maschile,
con negli occhi tiepidi il desiderio di morire.

Ah, la vide subito, colui
che non perdona.

Vide l'infinita capacità di obbedire
e l'infinita capacità di ribellarsi:
la chiamò a sé, e operò su lei
—che lo guardava fiduciosa
come un agnello guarda il suo giusto carnefice—
la consacrazione a rovescio, mentre
nel suo sguardo cadeva
la luce, e saliva un'ombra di pietà.

VII

Doesn't forgive!

There was a soul, among those that
still had to descend into life
—so many, and all alike, poor souls—
a soul, in the light of whose brown eyes,
in the modest forelock combed up by a maternal idea
of male beauty, burned
the desire to die.

He saw it at once, he
who does not forgive.

He said, "Come closer." He took it,
and like an artisan
up there in the worlds that precede life,
laid hands on its head
and pronounced the malediction.

It was an innocent clean soul,
like a little boy at his first communion,
wise in the wisdom of his ten years,
dressed in white, in a material
chosen by the maternal idea of male grace, with,
in his warm eyes, the desire to die.

Ah, he saw it at once, he
who does not forgive.

He saw the infinite capacity to obey
and the infinite capacity to rebel:
he called it to him—and as it looked
at him, trustful, like a lamb looking at
its rightful executioner, he performed on it
the consecration in reverse, while,
over the fading light of his gaze,
a shadow of compassion was rising.

«Tu scenderai nel mondo,
e sarai candido e gentile, equilibrato e fedele,
avrai un'infinita capacità di obbedire
e un'infinita capacità di ribellarti.
Sarai puro.
Perciò ti maledico.»

Vedo ancora il suo sguardo
pieno di pietà—e del leggero orrore
che si prova per colui che la incute,
—lo sguardo con cui si segue
chi va, senza saperlo, a morire,
e, per una necessità che domina chi sa e chi non sa,
non gli si dice nulla—
vedo ancora il suo sguardo,
mentre mi allontanavo
—dall'Eternità—verso la mia culla.

VIII

*(Conclusione funerea: con tavola sinottica—ad
uso della facitrice del «pezzo»—della mia
carriera di poeta, e uno sguardo profetico al
mare dei futuri millenni.)*

«Venni al mondo al tempo
dell'Analogica.
Operai
in quel campo, da apprendista.
Poi ci fu la Resistenza
e io
lottai con le armi della poesia.
Restaurai la Logica, e fui
un poeta civile.
Ora è il tempo
della Psicagogica.
Posso scrivere solo profetando

"You shall go down into the world,
and you shall be innocent, gentle, well-balanced, and faithful,
you shall have an infinite capacity to obey
and an infinite capacity to rebel.
You shall be pure.
Therefore I curse you."

I still see his gaze
full of pity—as well as the mild horror
that one shows for him who inspires it
—the gaze with which one follows
him who goes off, without knowing it, to die,
and, from a need that governs him who knows and him who doesn't,
no one says anything to him—
I still see his gaze,
as I was turning away
—from Eternity—toward my cradle.

VIII

*(Funereal conclusion: with synoptic table—for
use of the writer of the "piece"—of my
career as a poet, and a prophetic look at
the ocean of future millennia.)*

"I came into the world at the time
of the Analogic.
I labored
in that field, as an apprentice.
Then there was the Resistance
and I
fought with the weapons of poetry.
I reinstated Logic, and I was
a civil poet.
Now is the time
of the Psychagogic.
I can only write, prophesying

nel rapimento della Musica
per eccesso di seme o di pietà.»

*

«Se ora l'Analogica sopravvive
e la Logica è passata di moda
(e io con lei:
non ho più richiesta di poesia),
la Psicagogica
c'è
(ad onta della Demagogia
sempre più padrona
della situazione).
È così
che io posso scrivere Temi e Treni
e anche Profezie;
da poeta civile, ah sì, sempre!»

*

«Quanto al futuro, ascolti:
i suoi figli fascisti
veleggeranno
verso i mondi della Nuova Preistoria.
Io me ne starò là,
come colui che suo dannaggio sogna
sulle rive del mare
in cui ricomincia la vita.
Solo, o quasi, sul vecchio litorale
tra ruderi di antiche civiltà,
Ravenna
Ostia, o Bombay—è uguale—
con Dei che si scrostano, problemi vecchi
—quale la lotta di classe—
che
si dissolvono . . .
Come un partigiano
morto prima del maggio del '45,

in the rapture of Music
through an excess of seed or compassion."

*

"If now the Analogic survives
and Logic has passed out of fashion
(and I with it:
I'm no longer asked for poetry),
there is
the Psychagogic
(to the disgrace of the Demagogy
ever more in control
of the situation).
And thus
I can write Themes and Trains
and even Prophecies;
as a civil poet, ah yes, always!"

*

"As for the future, listen:
your fascist sons
will sail
toward the worlds of the New Prehistory.
I'll be there, but by myself,
like someone dreaming of his own damnation
on the shores of the sea
in which life begins again.
Alone, or almost, on the old coastline
among ruins of ancient civilizations,
Ravenna,
Ostia, or Bombay—it's all the same—
with gods that peel off, old problems
—such as class struggle—
which
dissolve . . .
Like a Partisan
dead before May 1945,

comincerò piano piano a decompormi,
    nella luce straziante di quel mare,
        poeta e cittadino dimenticato.»

   I X

                                           (Clausola)

«Dio mio, ma allora cos'ha
lei all'attivo? . . .»
«Io?—[un balbettio, nefando,
    non ho preso l'optalidon, mi trema la voce
        di ragazzo malato]—
Io? Una disperata vitalità.»

(1963)

I will begin little by little to decompose,
   in the tormenting light of that sea,
    as a poet and citizen, forgotten."

I X

     (End of Statement)

"My god, but then what can be said
in your favor? . . ."
"Me?"—[nefarious stammering
   I didn't take the aspirin, my trembling voice
     that of a sick boy]—
"Me? A desperate vitality."

   (1963)

Camminavo nei dintorni dell'albergo—era sera—
e quattro o cinque ragazzetti comparvero,
nella pelle di tigre dei prati, senza
una rupe, un buco, un po' di vegetazione
dove riparasi da eventuali spari: ché
Israele era lì, sulla stessa pelle di tigre,
cosparsa di case di cemento e vani
muretti, come in ogni periferia.
Li raggiunsi, in quell'assurdo punto,
lontano dalla strada, dall'albergo,
dal confine. Fu un'ennesima amicizia,
una di quelle che durando una sera,
straziano poi tutta la vita. Essi,
i diseredati, e, per di più, figli
(che, dei diseredati hanno il sapere
del male—il furto, la rapina, la menzogna—
e, dei figli, l'ingenua idealità
del sentirsi consacrare al mondo),
essi, ebbero subito la vecchia luce d'amore
—come gratitudine—nel fondo degli occhi.
E, parlando, parlando, finché
scese la notte (e già uno mi abbracciava,
dicendo ora che mi odiava, ora che no,
mi amava, mi amava), seppi, di loro, ogni cosa,
ogni semplice cosa. Questi erano gli dei
o figli di dei, che misteriosamente sparavano,
per un odio che li avrebbe spinti giù dai monti di creta,
come sposi assetati di sangue, sui Kibutz invasori
sull'altra metà di Gerusalemme . . .
Questi straccioni, che vanno a dormire, ora,
all'aperto, in fondo a un prato di periferia.
Coi loro fratelli maggiori, soldati
armati di un vecchio fucile e di due baffi
di mercenari rassegnati a vecchie morti.
Questi sono i Giordani terrore di Israele,
questi che davanti a me piangono
l'antico dolore dei profughi. Uno di essi,

I was walking near the hotel in the evening
when four or five boys appeared
on the field's tiger fur,
with no cliff, ditch, vegetation
to take cover from possible bullets—for
Israel was there, on the same tiger fur
specked with cement-block houses, useless
walls, like all slums.
I happened on them at that absurd point
far from street, hotel,
border. It was one of countless such
friendships, which last an evening
then torture the rest of your life. They,
the disinherited and, what's more, sons
(possessing the knowledge the disinherited
have of evil—burglary, robbery, lying—
and the naïve ideal sons have
of feeling consecrated to the world),
deep in their eyes, right off, was the old
light of love, almost gratitude.
And talking, talking till
night came (already one was embracing me,
saying now he hated me, now, no, he loved me,
loved me) they told me everything about themselves,
every simple thing. These were gods
or sons of gods, mysteriously shooting because
of a hate that would push them down from
the clay hills like bloodthirsty bridegrooms upon
the invading kibbutzim on the other side of Jerusalem . . .
These ragged urchins, who sleep in open air now
at the edge of a slum field—
with elder brothers, soldiers armed with
old rifles, mustached like those
destined to die the ancient deaths of mercenaries—
These are the Jordanians, terror of Israel,
weeping before my eyes
the ancient grief of refugees. One of them,

deputato all'odio, già quasi borghese (al moralismo
ricattatore, al nazionalismo che sbianca di furore
nevrotico) mi canta il vecchio ritornello
imparato dalla sua radio, dai suoi re—
un altro, nei suoi stracci, ascolta assentendo,
mentre, come un cucciolo, si stringe a me,
non provando altro, nel prato di confine,
nel deserto giordano, nel mondo,
che un misero sentimento di amore.

(1963)

sworn to a hate that's already almost bourgeois (to blackmailing
moralism, to nationalism that has paled with neurotic
fury), sings to me the old refrain
learned from his radio, from his kings—
another, in his rags, listens, agreeing,
while puppylike he presses close to me,
not showing, in a slum field
of the Jordan's desert, in the world,
anything but love's poor simple feeling.

(1963)

PROGETTO DI OPERE FUTURE

Anche oggi, nella malinconica fisicità
in cui la nazione è occupata a formare un Governo,
e il Centro-Sinistra ai fragili linguisti fa

fremere gli organi normativi—l'inverno
imbeve di oscura luce le cose lontane
e accende appena, mauve e verde, le vicine, in un esterno

perduto nel fondo delle età italiane . . .
con le terre azzurre di Piero sgorganti da indicibili
azzurrini di Linguadoca . . . se non da siciliane

azzurrità di Origini . . . che qui, nelle rozze appendici
degli squisiti Centri, sono verdi e mauve,
per fango e cielo, limoni e rose . . . occhi di Federici

con metà cuore in cerchi di mandorli rupestri dove
cade luce d'Arabia, l'altra metà in qualche avvallamento
imperlato di nebbia: con Alpi lontane, follemente nuove . .

Impazzisco! È tutta la vita che tento
di esprimere questo sgomento da Recherche
—che io sentivo già bambino, sul Tagliamento,

o sul Po, più vicino alle matrici—alla cerchia
dei miei isoglotti—sordi, per abitudine
a ogni privata, infantile, incerta

pre-espressività, dove il cuore sia nudo.
Ma io—fidando che qualcosa prima di morire
i mille miei tentativi portino ai giudici—

nell'epoca in cui l'italiano sta per finire
perduto da anglosassone o da russo,
torno, nudo, appunto, e pazzo, al verde aprile,

Even today, in this melancholy physicality
when the nation's occupied forming a government
and "Center-Left" causes the fragile linguists'

normative organs to shudder—winter steeps
distant objects in obscure light while barely
kindling mauve-green closer ones,

in an exterior lost deep in the Italian ages . . .
with Piero's azure earths arising out of Languedoc's
unsayable azurines . . . or perhaps the Sicilian

azurities of the Beginnings . . . which here in the rough
appendixes of the exquisite Centers, are green, mauve,
for mud, sky, lemons, roses . . . eyes of Fredericks,

half their heart in rings of rocky almond groves,
lit by Arabian sun; other half
in some fog-beaded valley, the distant Alps insanely new . . .

I'm going mad! All my life I've been trying
to express this dismay, like Proust
—which I felt even as a child on the Tagliamento,

or Po, closer to the matrixes—to the circle of
those who speak my language—who, from habit,
are deaf to every private, infantile, unsure

pre-expressivity, where the heart is naked.
But trusting that, before I die, my thousand
efforts might bring something to the judges,

in this epoch when Italian's about to end,
defeated by either Anglo-American or Russian,
I return naked, and, as I said, mad, to green April,

al verde aprile, dell'idioma illustre
(che mai fu, mai fu!), alto-italiano . . .
alla Verderbnis franco-veneta, lusso

di atticciate popolazioni fuori mano . . .
al verde aprile—con la modernità
d'Israele come un'ulcera nell'anima—

dove io Ebreo offeso da pietà,
ritrovo una crudele freschezza d'apprendista,
nelle vicende dell'altra (funebre) metà

della vita . . . Mi rifaccio cattolico, nazionalista,
romanico, nelle mie ricerche per «BESTEMMIA»,
o «LA DIVINA MIMESIS»—e, ah mistica

filologia!, nei giorni della vendemmia
gioisco come si gioisce seminando,
col fervore che opera mescolanze di materie

inconciliabili, magmi senza amalgama, quando
la vita è limone o rosa d'aprile.
Merde! Cercare di spiegare come vanno

le cose della lingua, senza inferire
concomitanze politiche! unità
linguistica senza ragioni di vile

interesse, senza l'insensibilità
di una classe che se ne frega di elezione
gergale-letteraria! Professori del ca.,

neo o paleo patrioti, teste coglione
in tanta scienza, che dal XII al XIV secolo
vedono solo testi in funzione

di altri testi . . . Basta: cieco
amore mio! Ti eserciterò in ricerche
translinguistiche, e a un testo opporrò un Veto,

to the green April of that illustrious language
(which, never was, never was!) High Italian . . .
to French-Venetian decadence, luxury

of stocky peripheral peoples . . .
to green April—with Israel's
modernity like an ulcer in the soul—

where I, Jew offended by pity, regain
an apprentice's cruel freshness in the events
of the other (funereal) half of life . . .

I transform myself back into a Catholic,
Nationalist, Romanesque, in my research for
"Blasphemy" or "The Divine Mimesis"—and, ah mystic

philology!, in the vintage days,
I rejoice as one rejoices sowing seed
with a fervor that mixes irreconcilable

substances, magmas without amalgam, when
life is April's lemon and rose.
Shit! To try to describe the condition

of language without assuming
political accompaniments! linguistic
unity without base economic

motives, without the insensibility
of a class that doesn't give a shit about slang-
literary choice! Fucking professors,

neo or paleo patriots, assholes up to their ears
in all that knowledge, who see twelfth- to fourteenth-
century texts only as functions

of other texts . . . Stop, my blind love!
I'll employ you in translinguistic
research, and to one text I'll oppose a veto,

e a tre testi tre Santi, e a una cerchia
letteraria tradizioni di cucina,
liti di confine: e nell'Anno della scoperta

di un testo omologato, da amanuensi di lingua patavina
per stupidità o vanità che sia, ricercherò
cosa facevano i pittori, di cascina in cascina

nella verde-sublime luce delle terre del Po . . .
ma soprattutto che cosa voleva
la classe al potere: una qualsiasi, che non so.

Ne comporrò un'opera mostruosa, coeva
alle Anti-opere, per lettera 22, della nuova moda,
vecchia figuratività nel fianco della giovane leva.

Ma bisogna deludere. Solo una nobile broda
d'ispirazioni miste, demistifica,
se miracolosamente il caos approda

a una plastica chiarezza, mettiamo, di grifi
romanici—coscioni, collottole, toraci
gonfi come pane, di pietra grigia che codifica

la piena Realtà. Taci, taci,
voce di ogni Ufficialità, qualunque tu sia.
Bisogna deludere. Saltare sulle braci

come martiri arrostiti e ridicoli: la via
della Verità passa anche attraverso i più orrendi
luoghi dell'estetismo, dell'isteria,

del rifacimento folle erudito. Splendidi,
per ragioni diverse da quelle romantico-
nazionalistiche, giorni delle prime vendite,

dei primi contratti! Se avrò poi cuore bastante
scriverò anche una «PASSIONALE STORIA
DELLA POESIA ITALIANA», oltre che un'ancora vacante

to three texts three saints, to a literary
circle, traditions of cooking, border
disputes; and in the year of the discovery

of a ratified text, by copyists
of the Paduan language, I'll search, driven by
stupidity or vanity, for what the painters were doing,

from farm to farm in the green-sublime light
of the lands of the Po . . . but above all for what
the ruling class wanted, whatever, I don't know.

I'll turn it into a monstrous work, contemporary
with the *lettera* 22's Anti-Works, very latest fashion,
old figurative mode stuck in the side of the young.

But one has to disappoint. Only a noble mishmash
of mixed inspirations can demystify
when chaos miraculously comes up on

a plastic clarity of, for instance, Romanesque
griffins—huge thighs, necks, and thoraxes
swollen like breadloaves, grey stone to codify

full Reality. Shut up, shut up, voices
of Everything Official, whatever you are.
One must disappoint . . . one must hop onto the coals

like roasted ridiculous martyrs: the Way
of Truth passes through even the most appalling
places of aestheticism, hysteria,

foolish erudite refashioning! Splendid
days (though not for the usual romantic-
nationalistic reasons), of first sales,

first contracts! If I have sufficient heart,
I'll also write "A Passionate History of
Italian Poetry," next to a still-blank

«MORTE DELLA POESIA» (ma io so, pieno di gloria
giovanile, che per me è ancora aprile,
son pieno di limoni e di rose . . .) In quella «STORIA»

(scritta in ottave, per ironia) «terrò a vile»
ogni precedente sistemazione, e, sotto il segno
primario di Marx, e quello, a seguire,

di Freud, ristabilirò nuove gerarchie nel regno
degli amori poetici: e alla esistenza
letteraria opporrò, col mio umiliato ingegno,

la nozione di Inespresso Esistente, senza
di cui ogni cosa è mistero:
finché non ci fu, così recente, la chiara coscienza

delle classi che dividono il mondo, il magistero
stilistico fu dominato sempre da ciò
che non poteva dire (o sapere): ma c'era.

Gioco dialettico sprofondato nel profondo, oh
sì!, da ricostruire stilema per stilema,
perché in ogni parola scritta nel Bel Paese dove il No

suona, c'era opposto allo stile quel Sema
imposseduto, la lingua di un popolo
che doveva ancora essere classe, problema

saputo e risolto solo in sogno. Fioco
per lungo silenzio brucerò poi in un «ALTRO MONOLOGO»
la rabbia impotente contro il mondo broccolo

tombale di Dallas, con un volo
di due versi per Kennedy, e una lassa
di settanta volte sette (mila) versi, per Coro

e Orchestra, con settantamila violini e una grancassa,
(e un disco di Bach), «CITAZIONE BRECHTIANA»
O «CANTI DELLA DISSACRAZIONE», che sia, melassa

"Death of Poetry" (but, filled with juvenile
glory, I know for me it's still April, I'm
full of lemons and roses . . .). In that "History"

(written in ottava rima, for irony) I'll
consider vile each previous systematization,
and under the primary signs of Marx and then of

Freud, I'll establish new hierarchies in the region
of poetic loves; and to the literary existence,
I'll oppose, with my humiliated talent,

the notion of the Unexpressed Existent,
without which everything's a mystery:
since, till recently, there was no clear

awareness of the classes that divide the world,
stylistic teaching was always dominated by
what it couldn't say (or know) but which existed.

Dialectical game diving deeper, oh yes, to be
rebuilt stileme after stileme, because in each
word written in the Bel Paese where the No

sounds, there was, opposed to the prevailing style,
that unpossessed Seme, Seed, the language of a people
who still had to become a class, a problem

known and resolved only in dreams. Then, faintly
because of long silence, in "Another Monologue,"
I'll burn with impotent rage against Dallas's

stupid graveyard world, with a flight of two
verses for Kennedy, and a loosing of seventy times
seven (thousand) verses, for chorus and orchestra,

with seventy thousand violins and a bass drum
(and a record of Bach), whether "Brechtian Quotation"
or "Desecration Cantos," pluralinguistic

plurilinguistica o matassa monolitica: in cui vana
apparirà TUTTA LA STORIA IN QUANTO OPERA DI PAZZI.
PAZZA FU L'ADOLFA PAZZA LA GIUSEPPA PAZZA L'ELITE [AMERICANA

PAZZA L'IDEOLOGIA PAZZE LE CHIESE PAZZI
I CAMPIONI DI IDEOLOGIE E DI CHIESE
CHE RICATTANO I BUONI E STUPIDI NORMALI PAZZI

I RIVOLUZIONARI PIENI DI BENPENSARE BORGHESE
CHE CONTINUANO SEMPLICEMENTE A ESSERE DEPOSITARI
DEL RICATTO MORALISTICO ALL'UOMO. Accese

dunque queste espressionistiche candele agli altari
del Sesso, tornerò alla Religione.
E scriverò all'imperterrito Moravia, una «PASOLINARIA

SUI MODI D'ESSER POETA», con la relazione
tra segno e cosa—e finalmente
svelerò la mia vera passione.

Che è la vita furente [o nolente] [o morente]
—e perciò, di nuovo, la poesia:
non conta né il segno né la cosa esistente,

ecco. Se l'uomo fosse un Monotipo nella Subtopia
di un mondo senza più capitali linguistiche,
e disparisse quindi la parola da ogni sua via

dell'udire e del dire, lo stringerebbero mistici
legami ancora alle cose, e ciò che le cose
sono, non fissato più nei tristi

contesti, sarebbe sempre nuovo, colmo di gaudiose
verità pragmatiche—non più strumentalità,
travaglio che le traduce in limoni, in rose . . .

ma sempre e solo, luce, com'è la realtà
delle cose quando sono nella memoria
alla soglia dell'essere nominate, e già

molasses or monolithic skein, in which ALL HISTORY
WILL SEEM VAIN INSOFAR AS IT'S THE WORK OF MADMEN.
MAD WAS ADOLPHA MAD JOSEPHA MAD THE AMERICAN ELITE

MAD IDEOLOGY MAD CHURCHES MAD
CHAMPIONS OF IDEOLOGIES AND CHURCHES
THAT BLACKMAIL GOOD AND STUPID NORMAL PEOPLE MAD

REVOLUTIONARIES WITH THEIR RIGHTEOUS BOURGEOIS THINKING
WHO CONTINUE TO BE SIMPLY DEPOSITARIES
OF THE MORALISTIC BLACKMAILING OF MAN. Then

once these expressionistic candles have been lit
at the altars of sex, I'll return to religion.
And to the undaunted Moravia I'll write a "Pasolinaria

on the Ways of Being a Poet," defining
the relationship between sign and thing—
and finally I'll reveal my true passion:

Which is life raging [or unwilling] [or dying]
—and thus, again poetry:
neither the sign nor the existing thing matters.

Yes. If man were a Monotype in the Subtopia
of a world with no linguistic capital cities anymore,
and then if the word disappeared from each

of his channels of hearing and saying,
mystical bonds would still tie him to things;
and that which things are, no longer fixed in their sad

contexts, would be always new, full of joyous
pragmatic truths—no longer instrumentality or
travail that translates them into lemons, roses . . .

but always and only light, as is the reality
of things when they are in the memory
at the threshold of being named and already

piene della loro fisica gloria.
Se poi dovessi scoprirmi un cancro, e crepare,
lo considererei una vittoria

di quella realtà di cose. Finita la pietà figliale
per il mondo, che senso ha ancora il frequentarlo?
Ah, non stare più in piedi nel sapore di sale

del mondo altrui (piccolo-borghese, letterario)
col bicchiere di whisky in mano e il viso di merda,
—ché mi dispiacerebbe solo non rappresentarlo

così com'è—prima che per me uomo si perda—
nella «DIVINA MIMESIS», opera, se mai ve ne fu,
da farsi, e, per mio strazio, così verde,

così verde, del verde d'una volta, della *mi joventud*,
nel mondaccio ingiallito della mia anima . . .
Ma no, ma no, è aprile, sono più

fresco d'un giovincello che ama
per le prime volte . . . Getterò giù presto, in tono
epistolare, con chiose e parentesi, una buriana

di «motivi accennati», di «eccetera», blasoni,
citazioni, e soprattutto allusività
(autoesortativi all'infinito e sproporzioni

di particolari in confronto al tutto), la
prima parodistica terzina fatta pagina magmatica
del Canto I, con fretta di giungere prima della prima metà,

là dove all'Inferno arcaico, enfatico
(romanico, come il centro delle nostre città
dal suburbio ormai per sempre spacciato)

s'inserisce un inserto d'Inferno dell'età
neocapitalistica, per nuovi tipi
di peccati (eccessi nella Razionalità

full of their physical glory. If I then
discovered a cancer in myself and died,
I'd consider it a victory of that reality

of things. Once filial piety for the world
is gone, why still frequent it?
Ah, not to need to stand anymore, bitterly,

in other people's worlds (petit-bourgeois, literary),
glass of whiskey in hand, shit-faced
(I'd be unhappy only in not presenting it as

it really is), before it's lost to me as a man,
in "The Divine Mimesis," a work to finish
if ever one was, and, for my torment, so green,

so green with the green of another time, of *mi joventud*,
in the ugly yellowed world of my soul . . .
But no, no, it's April, I'm fresher than

a young man in love for the first few times . . .
Soon I'll dash off, in epistolary tone,
with notes and parentheses, a devil's dance

of "hinted-at motives," "et ceteras," blazons,
quotations, and, above all, allusions
(infinite self-exhortations and disproportions

of details in relation to the whole), the first
parodistic tercet turned into magmatic page
of Canto I, rushing to insert, before the first half

ends, into the vivid archaic Inferno
(Romanesque, like the center of our cities
whose outskirts have been by now destroyed forever),

an insert of the neocapitalistic age's
Inferno for new types of sins
(excesses in Rationality and Irrationality)

e nell'Irrazionalità) a integrazione degli antichi.
E lì vedrai, in una edilizia di delizioso cemento,
riconoscendovi gli amici e i nemici,

sotto i cartelli segnaletici dell' «OPERA INCREMENTO
PENE INFERNALI», A: I TROPPO CONTINENTI: Conformisti
(salotto Bellonci), Volgari (un ricevimento

al Quirinale), Cinici (un convegno di giornalisti
del Corriere della Sera e affini): e poi:
i Deboli, gli Ambigui, i Paurosi (individualisti

questi, a casa loro); B: GLI INCONTINENTI, ZONA
PRIMA: eccesso di Rigore (socialisti borghesi,
piccoli benpensanti che si credono piccoli eroi,

solo per l'eroica scelta d'una buona bandiera), eccesso
di Rimorso (Soldati, Piovene); eccesso di Servilità
(masse infinite senza anagrafe, senza nome, senza sesso);

ZONA SECONDA: Raziocinanti (Landolfi) gente che sta
seduta sola nel suo cesso; Irrazionali
(l'intera avanguardia internazionale che va

dagli Endoletterari [De Gaulle] alle vestali
di Pound teutoniche o italiote);
Razionali (Moravia, rara avis, e le ali

degli Impegnati neo-gotici)
Oh, cecità dell'amore!
Lo vidi su due umili gote,

su due occhi di cucciolo: era amore,
perché sorriso, era una bambina
che correva in cuore al sole—

nella cecità del suo amore—dritta, meschina,
con quelle gabbanucce stracciate,
sotto un enorme acquedotto, su una banchina

to be integrated with the ancient ones.
And there you'll see, in a building of delectable cement,
recognizing friends and enemies,

under placards reading *"Corporation for Incrementation
of Infernal Punishments,"* A: *The Over-Continent*:
Conformists (Bellonci salon), the Vulgar (reception

at the Quirinale), the Cynics (get-together of journalists
from *Corriere della Sera* and by-products); and then
the Weak, Ambiguous, Fearful (these,

individualists only at home): B: *The Incontinent, First
Zone*: excessive Rigor (petty self-righteous bourgeois
socialists who think they're little heroes, merely

because they've heroically chosen a good flag); excessive
Remorse (Soldati, Piovene); excessive Servility
(infinite undocumented nameless sexless masses);

Second Zone: The Reasoning (Landolfi) people who stay
seated all alone, in the toilet; the Irrational
(the entire international avant-garde stretching

from the Endo-Literary [De Gaulle] to Pound's
Teutonic and Italian-born vestals);
the Rational (Moravia, rara avis,

and the wings of the neogothic *Engagé*)
Oh, love's blindness!
I saw it on two humble cheeks,

in two puppy eyes: it was love
because it was a smile, a little girl
running in the sunlight's heart

in her love's blindness, erect,
wretched in her tattered dress,
under an enormous aqueduct, on a mud

di fango, tra le baracche incatramate,
—che correva, la bambina, nel cuore
del sole, dritta, con le pupille attirate

per cecità di un umile, unico amore,
verso un'altra creatura bambina
che correva verso di lei, nel sole

degli abituri dove era madre, lei—meschina,
nel suo cappotto stracciato,
e correva, creatura verso la creaturina,

col sorriso complice, suscitato
insieme all'altro da uno stesso amore.
Correvano una verso l'altra con l'occhio legato

da quel contemporaneo sorriso nel sole.

Oh Marx—tutto è oro—oh Freud—tutto
è amore—oh Proust—tutto è memoria—
oh Einstein—tutto è fine—oh Charlot—tutto

è uomo—oh Kafka—tutto è terrore—
oh popolazione dei miei fratelli—
oh patria—oh ciò che rassicura l'identità—

oh pace che consente il selvaggio dolore—
oh marchio dell'infanzia! Oh destino d'oro
costruito sull'eros e sulla morte, come

una distrazione—e i suoi mille pretesti
il riso, la filosofia! Avere illusioni (l'amore)
differenzia, ma in una cerchia consacrata da testi

insostituibili. Torno con Israele in cuore,
soffrendo per i suoi figli-fratelli la nostalgia
dell'Europa romanza, occitanica, con lo spendore

un po' ingiallito ma pieno di un'atroce poesia
delle sue capitali borghesi sui fiumi o sui mari . . .
Norma negativa d'amore. La vera via

path between hovels smeared with tar
—girl running in the heart
of the sunlight, erect, her pupil

drawn by the blindness of a humble
unique love to another little girl
running toward her, in the sunlight

of humble dwellings where she was a mother,
wretched in her ragged dress,
darling running toward little darling,

with an accomplice's smile, aroused,
like the other's smile, by the same love.
Running each to each, their eyes bound up

by that simultaneous sunlit smile.

Oh Marx—all is gold—oh Freud—all
is love—oh Proust—all is memory—
oh Einstein—all is end—oh Chaplin—all

is man—oh Kafka—all is terror—
oh population of my brothers—
oh fatherland—oh that which reassures identity—

oh peace permitting savage pain—
oh mark of infancy! Oh destiny of gold
constructed on eros and death, as a

distraction—and its thousand pretexts:
laughter, philosophy! To have illusions (love)
sets one apart, but only within a circle consecrated by

irreplaceable texts. My heart full of Israel, I return home,
suffering for her sons and brothers, nostalgia
for Romance-language Europe, Occitanic, its splendor

somewhat yellowed though filled with the atrocious
poetry of its bourgeois capitals on rivers and seas . . .
Negative rule of love. For those who wish to

di chi vuol essere è deludere. Il che fa uguali
tutti fra loro, come i morti:
ma rimette in discussione i sacrali

testi delle cerchie. Perciò, aspettando che porti
un nuovo Grande Ebreo un nuovo TUTTO È
—a cui il mondo sputtanato si rivolti—

bisogna deludere, nel nostro piccolo ... Eh!,
bisogna abbandonare il proprio bel posto al sole
(e voi dovete lasciare Israele, Ebrei!

ché la cecità dell'amore
retrocede le invenzioni a istituzioni,
per reinventare poi solo col cuore;

e combina addirittura nazioni
con l'omertà d'una mamma e una figlietta al sole
—perseguitando, no?, le opposizioni ...)

Quanto a me, tendo pur'io (rabbia) a tale amore,
religione d'un elegiaco figlio,
che vuole a tutti costi farsi onore.

Né si esaurisce peraltro nel groviglio
di vita successa e da succedere: vuole
ridurre tutto al suo ordine di giglio.

Basta, c'è da ridere. Ah oscure
tortuosità che spingono a un «destino d'opposizione»!
Ma non c'è altra alternativa alle mie opere future.

«OPPOSIZIONE PURA», «PAPA GIOVANNI», O «PASSIONE
(O ARCHIVIO) DEGLI ANNI SESSANTA», che sia,
l'organo dove prima depositerò, in visione

semiprivata, si sa, tali mie opere future, appare come via
senza alternative, a me e alla redazione
degli imberbi deputati all'impegno—picciola compagnia

truly be, the true way is to undeceive—
which makes everyone the same as everyone else,
like the dead, but throws back into doubt the holy

texts of the circles. So, waiting for a new
Great Jew to inaugurate a new ALL IS
—which the wicked world will turn against—

one must undeceive in our little . . . Yes!
one must abandon one's beautiful place in the sun
(and you must leave Israel, Jews!

since love's blindness
reduces inventions to institutions
and then reinvents only with the heart

and even mixes nations together, with the silent
sunlit complicity of a mama and her little daughter
—persecuting the oppositions—right?).

As for me, I myself lean (in rage) toward
such love, religion of an elegiac son
who wishes at all costs to distinguish himself.

Nor does he exhaust himself in the tangle
of past and future life but wishes most
to reduce everything to his order of a lily.

No, I've been joking. Oh intricate dark
twists that push one to a "destiny of opposition"!
But there's no other alternative to my future works.

Whether it's *Pure Opposition, Pope John,*
or *Passion (or Archive) of the Sixties,*
the organ where I'll first deposit, for semiprivate

viewing, such future works of mine, appears as
the only alternative to me and the board
of beardless editors delegated to the task—tiny corps

che vuol sapere: quasi per elezione
di seme. Opposizione di chi non può
essere amato da nessuno, e nessuno può amare, e pone

quindi il suo amore come un no
prestabilito, esercizio del dovere
politico come esercizio di ragione.
                                    Infine, ah lo so,

mai, nella mia malridotta passione,
mai fui tanto cadavere come ora
che riprendo in mano le mie tabulae presentiae—

se reale è la realtà, ma dopo
ch'è stata distrutto nell'eterno e nell'ora
dall'ossessa idea di un nulla lucente.*

Ma in questa realtà—la nostra—
ansimante dietro i destini delle strutture,
—per ritardo, per ritardo, nella mora

mortuale d'un'epochetta precedente—
o in anticipo, per dolore della fine
del mondo come sua impossibile cessazione—

accerto un bisogno struggente
di minoranze alleate. Tornate, Ebrei,
agli albori di questa Preistoria,

che alla maggioranza sorride come Realtà:
perdita dell'umanità e ricostituzione
culturale del nuovo uomo—dicono

gli intenditori. E infatti la cosa è qua:
nell'atmosfera d'una piccola nazione,
che nella fattispecie è l'Italia—si dà

* fr. il vers. «non conta né il segno né la cosa esistente».

that wants knowledge, as though by birthright.
Opposition of one who can't
be loved by anyone, and who can't love anyone, and therefore

sets his love as a pre-established
no, exercise of political
duty as exercise of reason.
                              In the end, oh I know,

never, in my haggard passion,
have I ever been such a cadaver as now
as I take again in hand my tables of the present—

if reality's real, but after it's been
destroyed in the eternal and the moment by
the obsessive idea of a shining nothingness.*

But in this our reality, either breathlessly
pursuing the destinies of structures
—in a deathly extension

of the preceding minor period—or in
anticipatory grief for the end of the world
as its impossible cessation—

I verify the heartrending need for
allied minorities. Come back, Jews,
to the dawn of this Prehistory,

which for the majority smiles like Reality
and for the connoisseurs is
loss of humanity and cultural reconstitution

of the new man. And, in fact, here's the point:
in the atmosphere of a small nation,
in this case, Italy—a false dilemma

---

 * [Note by Pasolini] Compare the line "neither the sign nor the existing thing
matters."

un falso dilemma tra la Rivoluzione e un'Entità
che vien detta Centrosinistra—con rossore
dei Linguisti . . . Il nuovo corso della realtà

è così ammesso e accettato. Tornate,
Ebrei, a contraddirlo, coi quattro
gatti che hanno finalmente chiarito

il loro destino: va verso il futuro
il Potere, e lo segue, nell'atto trionfante,
l'Opposizione, potere nel potere.

Per chi è crocifisso alla sua razionalità straziante,
macerato dal puritanesimo, non ha più senso
che un'aristocratica, e ahi, impopolare opposizione.

La rivoluzione non è più che un sentimento.

(Novembre–Dicembre 1963)

is posed between Revolution and an Entity
called the Center-Left—making
the linguists blush . . . the new course of reality

is thus admitted and accepted. Return,
Jews, to contradict it, with those
few who've finally clarified

their destiny: Power goes toward
the future, and the Opposition follows it, in
the act of its triumph, power within power.

For one crucified to his tormenting rationality,
butchered by puritanism, nothing makes sense anymore
but an aristocratic and alas unpopular opposition.

The revolution is now just a sentiment.

(November–December 1963)

TO TRANSFIGURE, TO ORGANIZE

(1971)

PART FOUR

Ohi, Ninarieddo, ti ricordi di quel sogno . . .
di cui abbiamo parlato tante volte . . .
Io ero in macchina, e partivo solo, col sedile
vuoto accanto a me, e tu mi correvi dietro;
all'altezza dello sportello ancora semiaperto,
correndo ansioso e ostinato, mi gridavi
con un po' di pianto infantile nella voce:
«A Pa', mi porti con te? Me lo paghi il viaggio?»
Era il viaggio della vita: e solo in sogno
hai dunque osato scoprirti e chiedermi qualcosa.
Tu sai benissimo che quel sogno fa parte della realtà;
e non è un Ninetto sognato quello che ha detto quelle parole.
Tanto è vero che quando ne parliamo arrossisci.
Ieri sera, a Arezzo, nel silenzio della notte,
mentre il piantone rinchiudeva con la catena il cancello
alle tue spalle, e tu stavi per sparire,
col tuo sorriso, fulmineo e buffo, mi hai detto . . . «Grazie!».
«Grazie», Ninè? È la prima volta che me lo dici.
E infatti te ne accorgi, e ti correggi, senza perdere la faccia
(cosa in cui sei maestro) scherzando:
«Grazie per il passaggio.» Il viaggio che tu volevi
ch'io ti pagassi era, ripeto, il viaggio della vita:
è in quel sogno di tre quattro anni fa che ho deciso
ciò a cui il mio equivoco amore per la libertà era contrario.
Se ora mi ringrazi per il passaggio . . . Dio mio,
mentre tu sei in gattabuia, prendo con paura
l'aereo per un luogo lontano. Della nostra vita sono insaziabile,
perché una cosa unica al mondo non può essere mai esaurita.

(Settembre 2, 1969)

Hey Ninetto, remember that dream
we've talked about so many times? . . .
I was in the car, driving off alone, the seat
beside me empty, and you were running behind me;
next to the still-half-open door,
running anxious, obstinate, you were shouting,
with a childish wail in your voice:
"Hey Paul, take me with you? Will you pay my way?"
It was the journey of life: and so only in a dream
did you dare reveal yourself and ask me for something.
You know very well that dream is part of reality,
and it is no dreamed Ninetto who spoke those words.
In fact, when we speak of it, you blush.
Last evening, in Arezzo, in the silence of the night,
as the sentry closed the gate behind you
with the chain, and you were about to vanish,
with your flash of a funny smile, you said to me: "Thanks!"
"Thanks," Niño? It's the first time you said that to me.
And, in fact, you realize it and correct yourself, without losing face
(something you're a master of), joking:
"Thanks for the ride." The journey you wanted
me to pay for was, I repeat, the journey of life:
it was in that dream of three or four years ago that I decided
what was the opposite of my ambiguous love for freedom.
Now when you thank me for the ride . . . My God,
while you're in jail, I fearfully take
the plane for a distant place. I'm insatiable for our life,
because something unique in all the world can never be exhausted.

(September 2, 1969)

Le loro guancie erano fresche e tenere
e forse erano baciate per la prima volta.
Visti di spalle, quando le voltavano
per tornare nel tenero gruppo, erano più adulti,
coi cappotti sopra i calzoni leggeri. La loro povertà
dimentica che è il freddo inverno. Le gambe un po' arcuate
e i colletti consunti, come i fratelli maggiori,
già screditati cittadini. Essi sono ancora per qualche anno
senza prezzo: e non ci può essere niente che umilia
in chi non si può giudicare. Per quanto lo facciano
con tanta, incredibile naturalezza, essi si offrono alla vita;
e la vita a sua volta li richiede. Ne sono così pronti!
Restituiscono i baci, saggiando la novità.
Poi se ne vanno, imperturbati come sono venuti.
Ma poiché sono ancora pieni di fiducia in quella vita che li ama,
fanno sincere promesse, progettano un promettente futuro
di abbracci e anche baci. Chi farebbe la rivoluzione—
se mai la si dovesse fare—se non loro? Diteglielo: sono pronti,
tutti allo stesso modo, così come abbracciano e baciano
e con lo stesso odore nelle guancie.
Ma non sarà la loro fiducia nel mondo a trionfare.
Essa deve essere trascurata dal mondo.

(Dicembre 1969)

Their cheeks were fresh and tender,
perhaps kissed for the first time.
Seen from behind, as they turned
to rejoin their tender group, they looked older,
coats over light trousers. Their poverty
ignores the winter's cold. Slightly bowlegged . . .
collars ragged . . . like their older brothers,
already discredited citizens. For a few more years
they won't have a price, and nothing can humiliate
those unable to judge themselves. Though they do it
with so much incredible spontaneity, they're offering themselves to life,
and life in turn needs them. They're so ready for it!
They return the kisses, savoring the novelty.
Then they go, as imperturbably as when they came.
But since they're still confident of that life that
cherishes them, they make sincere promises, plan a promising future
of embraces, even kisses. Who would make the revolution—
if it ever took place—but they? Tell them; they're ready,
as one man, as they embrace and kiss,
with the same aroma in their cheeks.
But it won't be their trust in the world that triumphs.
That the world will have to overlook.

(December 1969)

La solitudine: bisogna essere molto forti
per amare la solitudine; bisogna avere buone gambe
e una resistenza fuori del comune; non si deve rischiare
raffreddore, influenza o mal di gola; non si devono temere
rapinatori o assassini; se tocca camminare
per tutto il pomeriggio o magari per tutta la sera
bisogna saperlo fare senza accorgersene; da sedersi non c'è;
specie d'inverno; col vento che tira sull'erba bagnata,
e coi pietroni tra l'immondizia umidi e fangosi;
non c'è proprio nessun conforto, su ciò non c'è dubbio,
oltre a quello di avere davanti tutto un giorno e una notte
senza doveri o limiti di qualsiasi genere.
Il sesso è un pretesto. Per quanti siano gli incontri
—e anche d'inverno, per le strade abbandonate al vento,
tra le distese d'immondizia contro i palazzi lontani,
essi sono molti—non sono che momenti della solitudine;
più caldo e vivo è il corpo gentile
che unge di seme e se ne va,
più freddo e mortale è intorno il diletto deserto;
è esso che riempie di gioia, come un vento miracoloso,
non il sorriso innocente o la torbida prepotenza
di chi poi se ne va; egli si porta dietro una giovinezza
enormemente giovane; e in questo è disumano,
perché non lascia traccie, o meglio, lascia una sola traccia
che è sempre la stessa in tutte le stagioni.
Un ragazzo ai suoi primi amori
altro non è che la fecondità del mondo.
È il mondo che così arriva con lui; appare e scompare,
come una forma che muta. Restano intatte tutte le cose,
e tu potrai percorrere mezza città, non lo ritroverai più;
l'atto è compiuto, la sua ripetizione è un rito. Dunque
la solitudine è ancora più grande se una folla intera
attende il suo turno: cresce infatti il numero delle sparizioni—
l'andarsene è fuggire—e il seguente incombe sul presente
come un dovere, un sacrificio da compiere alla voglia di morte.
Invecchiando, però, la stanchezza comincia a farsi sentire,
specie nel momento in cui è appena passata l'ora di cena,

LINES FROM THE TESTAMENT

Solitude: you must be very strong
to love solitude; you have to have good legs
and uncommon resistance; you must avoid catching
colds, flu, sore throat; and you must not fear
thieves and murderers; if you have to walk
all afternoon or even all evening
you must do it with ease; there's no sitting down,
especially in winter, with wind striking the wet grass,
and damp mud-caked stone slabs among garbage;
there's no real consolation, none at all,
beyond having a whole day and night ahead of you
with absolutely no duties or limits.
Sex is a pretext. For however many the encounters
—and even in winter, through streets abandoned to the wind,
amid expanses of garbage against distant buildings,
there are many—they're only moments in the solitude;
the livelier and warmer the sweet body
that anoints with seed and then departs,
the colder and deathlier the beloved desert around you;
like a miraculous wind, it fills you with joy,
it, not the innocent smile or troubled arrogance
of the one who then goes away; he carries with him a youthfulness
awesomely young; and in this he's inhuman
because he leaves no traces, or, better, only one trace
that's always the same in all seasons.
A boy in his first loves
is nothing less than the world's fecundity.
It is the world that thus arrives with him, appearing, disappearing,
like a changing form. All things remain the same—
and you'll search half the city without finding him again;
the deed is done; its repetition is ritual. And
the solitude's still greater if a whole crowd
waits its turn: in fact the number of disappearances grows—
leaving is fleeing—and what follows weighs upon the present
like a duty, a sacrifice performed to the death wish.
Growing old, however, one begins to feel weary
especially at the moment when dinnertime is over

e per te non è mutato niente; allora per un soffio non urli o piangi;
e ciò sarebbe enorme se non fosse appunto solo stanchezza,
e forse un po' di fame. Enorme, perché vorrebbe dire
che il tuo desiderio di solitudine non potrebbe esser più soddisfatto,
e allora cosa ti aspetta, se ciò che non è considerato solitudine
è la solitudine vera, quella che non puoi accettare?
Non c'è cena o pranzo o soddisfazione del mondo,
che valga una camminata senza fine per le strade povere,
dove bisogna essere disgraziati e forti, fratelli dei cani.

(1969)

and for you nothing is changed; then you're near to screaming or weeping;
and that would be awesome if it wasn't precisely merely weariness
and perhaps a little hunger. Awesome, because that would mean
your desire for solitude could no longer be satisfied,
and if what isn't considered solitude is the true solitude,
the one you can't accept, what can you expect?
There's no lunch or dinner or satisfaction in the world
equal to an endless walk through the streets of the poor,
where you must be wretched and strong, brothers to the dogs.

(1969)

Oh generazione sfortunata!
Cosa succederà domani, se tale classe dirigente—
quando furono alle prime armi
non conobbero la poesia della tradizione
ne fecero un'esperienza infelice perché senza
sorriso realistico gli fu inaccessibile
e anche per quel poco che la conobbero, dovevano dimostrare
di voler conoscerla sì ma con distacco, fuori dal gioco.
Oh generazione sfortunata!
che nell'inverno del '70 usasti cappotti e scialli fantasiosi
e fosti viziata
chi ti insegnò a non sentirti inferiore—
rimuovesti le tue incertezze divinamente infantili—
chi non è aggressivo è nemico del popolo! Ah!
I libri, i vecchi libri passarono sotto i tuoi occhi
come oggetti di un vecchio nemico
sentisti l'obbligo di non cedere
davanti alla bellezza nata da ingiustizie dimenticate
fosti in fondo votata ai buoni sentimenti
da cui ti difendevi come dalla bellezza
con l'odio razziale contro la passione;
venisti al mondo, che è grande eppure così semplice,
e vi trovasti chi rideva della tradizione,
e tu prendesti alla lettera tale ironia fintamente ribalda,
erigendo barriere giovanili contro la classe dominante del passato
la gioventù passa presto; oh generazione sfortunata,
arriverai alli mezza età e poi alla vecchiaia
senza aver goduto ciò che avevi diritto di godere
e che non si gode senza ansia e umiltà
e così capirai di aver servito il mondo
contro cui con zelo «portasti avanti la lotta»:
era esso che voleva gettar discredito sopra la storia—la sua;
era esso che voleva far piazza del passato—il suo;
oh generazione sfortunata, e tu obbedisti disobbedendo!
Era quel mondo a chiedere ai suoi nuovi figli di aiutarlo
a contraddirsi, per continuare;
vi troverete vecchi senza l'amore per i libri e la vita:

THE POETRY OF THE TRADITION

Oh unfortunate generation!
What will happen tomorrow, if whatever ruling class—
when they were fledglings
they didn't know the poetry of the tradition
their experience of it was unhappy because since they
lacked a realistic smile it was beyond them
and even for what little of it they came to know, they had to show
they wanted to know it yes but as detached spectators.
Oh unfortunate generation!
who in the winter of '70 wore fanciful overcoats and shawls
and were spoiled
who taught you not to feel inferior—
you repressed your divinely infantile uncertainties—
he who's not aggressive is an enemy of the people! Ah!
The books, the old books passed before your eyes
like the belongings of an old enemy
you felt obligated not to yield
to beauty grown in the soil of forgotten injustices
you were in the end devoted to good sentiments
against which you defended yourselves as against that beauty
with a racist's hate against passion;
you came into the world, which is vast and yet so simple,
and encountered those who laughed at the tradition,
and you took literally that mock-ribald irony,
erecting juvenile barriers against the ruling class of the past,
youth passes soon; oh unfortunate generation,
you'll become middle-aged, then old
without enjoying what you had the right to enjoy
and can't be enjoyed without anxiety and humility
and thus you'll realize you've served the world
against which, so zealously, you "carried on the struggle":
it was that world that wanted to discredit history—its;
it wanted to wipe the slate clean of the past—its;
oh unfortunate generation, and you obeyed by disobeying!
It was that world which asked its new children to help it
contradict itself, in order to continue;
you'll find yourselves old, without a love of books and life:

perfetti abitanti di quel mondo rinnovato
attraverso le sue reazioni e repressioni, sì, sì, è vero,
ma soprattutto attraverso voi, che vi siete ribellati
proprio come esso voleva, Automa in quanto Tutto;
non vi si riempirono gli occhi di lacrime
contro un Battistero con caporioni e garzoni
intenti di stagione in stagione
né lacrime aveste per un'ottava del Cinquecento,
né lacrime (intellettuali, dovute alla pura ragione)
non conosceste o non riconosceste i tabernacoli degli antenati
né le sedi dei padri padroni, dipinte da
—e tutte le altre sublimi cose
non vi farà trasalire (con quelle lacrime brucianti)
il verso di un anonimo poeta simbolista morto nel
la lotta di classe vi cullò e vi impedì di piangere:
irrigiditi contro tutto ciò che non sapesse di buoni sentimenti
e di aggressività disperata
passaste una giovinezza
e, se eravate intellettuali,
non voleste dunque esserlo fino in fondo,
mentre questo era poi fra i tanti il vostro vero dovere,
e perché compiste questo tradimento?
per amore dell'operaio: ma nessuno chiede a un operaio
di non essere operaio fino in fondo
gli operai non piansero davanti ai capolavori
ma non perpetrarono tradimenti che portano al ricatto
e quindi all'infelicità
oh sfortunata generazione
piangerai, ma di lacrime senza vita
perché forse non saprai neanche riandare
a ciò che non avendo avuto non hai neanche perduto;
povera generazione calvinista come alle origini della borghesia
fanciullescamente pragmatica, puerilmente attiva
tu hai cercato salvezza nell'organizzazione
(che non può altro produrre che altra organizzazione)
e hai passato i giorni della gioventù
parlando il linguaggio della democrazia burocratica
non uscendo mai dalla ripetizione delle formule,
chè organizzar significar per verba non si poria,
ma per formule sì,
ti troverai a usare l'autorità paterna in balia del potere

perfect inhabitants of that world renewed
through its reactions and repressions, yes, yes, it's true,
but above all through you, who rebelled,
just as it wanted, an Automaton because Unanimous;
your eyes didn't fill with tears
against a Baptistry of masters and apprentices
intent from season to season
you didn't weep for a fourteenth-century octave
you didn't even know what tears were (intellectuals, in hock to
pure reason), you didn't recognize your ancestors' tabernacles
or the headquarters of boss fathers, painted by
and all those other sublime things
you won't be astonished (with those burning tears)
by the lines of an anonymous symbolist poet who died in the
the class struggle lulled you, prevented you from weeping:
hardened against anything that didn't ooze the right sentiments
and desperate aggressiveness
you spent your youth
and, if you were intellectuals
you didn't want to see that through—
though this was your true duty, among many others,
and why did you commit this treason?
for the sake of the workers; but no one asks a worker
not to be a worker all the way
the workers didn't weep in front of masterworks
but they didn't perpetrate treasons leading to blackmail
and thus unhappiness
oh unfortunate generation
you'll weep, but lifeless tears
because perhaps you won't even know how to return to
what, not having had, you couldn't even lose;
poor Calvinist generation as at the bourgeoisie's origins
adolescently pragmatic, childishly active
you sought salvation in organization
(which can't produce anything but more organization)
and you've spent the days of your youth
speaking the jargon of bureaucratic democracy
never departing from the repetition of formulas,
for organizing can be signified not through words
but through formulas, yes,
you'll find yourselves using the same paternal authority,

imparlabile che ti ha voluta contro il potere,
generazione sfortunata!
Io invecchiando vidi le vostre teste piene di dolore
dove vorticava un'idea confusa, un'assoluta certezza,
una presunzione di eroi destinati a non morire—
oh ragazzi sfortunati, che avete visto a portata di mano
una meravigliosa vittoria che non esisteva!

   (1970)

at the mercy of that ineffable power that willed you against power,
unfortunate generation!
Growing old, I saw your heads fill with grief
where a confused idea swirled, an absolute certainty,
an assumption of heroes destined not to die—
oh unfortunate young people, who've seen within reach
a marvelous victory that didn't exist!

(1970)

My last book of verses, *Poetry in the Form of a Rose,* was published six years ago, in 1964. Since then, I've made many films (from *The Gospel According to Saint Matthew,* which I was working on when *Poetry in the Form of a Rose* appeared, to *Hawks and Sparrows, Oedipus Rex, Teorema, Porcile,* and *Medea*);* I made all these films "as a poet."[1] It's not necessary here to analyze the equivalence between the "poetic feeling" aroused by certain sequences in my films and a similar one aroused by certain parts of my books of poetry. The attempt to define such an equivalence has never been made except very generally, when referring to subject matter. But I think one can't deny that *a certain way of feeling something* occurs *in the same identical way* when one is faced with some of my lines and some of my shots.

But, since 1964 I've written poems not solely through film; for only a year or two was I silent as a "verse poet" (though even then I wrote things that have never been published or have remained incomplete); in 1965 I was confined to bed for a month, and during my convalescence I started working again, and—perhaps because during my illness I'd been rereading Plato with an indescribable joy—I began writing plays: six tragedies in verse that I've continued working on for the last five years—sometimes going back to them after a year or more away from them . . . and which will soon be published under the title *Calderón.*†

Obviously, at that time I was able to write poetry only by attributing it to characters who could act as my intermediaries.

But I began again with a few occasional poems, some even written on commission—after a first piece that wasn't much revised—"The Italian Communist Party Speaks to the Young!!"—written in the first days of March 1968 and pub-

---

Translators' note: This essay is the introduction to a paperback selection (Garzanti, 1970) of Pasolini's poems collected by him from three earlier books: *The Ashes of Gramsci, The Religion of My Time,* and *Poetry in the Form of a Rose.* The numbered footnotes are Pasolini's.

* His other feature-length films are *Accattone* (1961), *Mamma Roma* (1962), *La Ricotta* (1963), *The Decameron* (1970), *Canterbury Tales* (1972), *Arabian Nights* (1974), and *Salò: The 120 Days of Sodom* (1975).

[1] I use this word in its strictly "technical" sense.

† Only four of the plays have so far been published in Italian: *Pilade* (1967), *Orgia* and *Affabulazione* (both 1969), and *Calderón* (1973), all in separate volumes.

lished soon after, treacherously, without my knowledge, in a photo journal.[2] In the autumn of that year, I began again to be a maker of verses in the usual sense of the word; and now I have a new volume ready, *To Transfigure, To Organize*, to be brought out soon by the same publisher for whom I'm writing this introduction to my "old" poems.

Six years isn't a long period; but if one remembers that the first of the volumes excerpted here appeared in June 1957 (and its title poem, "The Ashes of Gramsci," dates from May 1954), then the six-year interval in fact represents an entire literary and political epoch (although—at least partly, with the last poems— lived in transition).

I therefore believe I'm addressing a "new reader." And I want simply to give him information, which is in fact all I'm capable of giving him.

I didn't begin writing poetry with "The Ashes of Gramsci"; I began much earlier—specifically in 1929 in Sacile,* when I was barely seven, in the second grade.

It was my mother who showed me how poetry could be written and not just read in school. One fine day, mysteriously, she presented me with a sonnet she'd composed in which she expressed her love for me (I don't know through which contortions of rhyme the poem ended with the words "of love for you I've lots"). A few days later, I wrote my first verses, in which I spoke of a "nightingale" and "bosky dell." I don't believe at that time I could have told a nightingale from a finch, or even an elm from a poplar, and, in any case, we certainly didn't read Petrarch in school (in that unforgettable second-grade class with my teacher, Mrs. Ada Costella, a Tuscan). So I don't know where I learned the classical code of linguistic election and selection. But the fact remains that, not taking into account my mother's abundant heart, I began as rigidly "selective" and "elect."

Since then, I've written entire collections of verse: at thirteen I was an epic poet (from the *Iliad* to the *Lusiads*). I didn't overlook verse drama. I didn't avoid, in my adolescence, the inevitable encounter with Carducci, Pascoli, D'Annunzio, a phase that had begun in Scandiano (as a commuter I attended the *ginnasio* of Reggio Emilia) and ended in Bologna at the Liceo Galvani, in 1937, when the substitute teacher, Antonio Rinaldi, read a poem by Rimbaud to the class.

From 1937 to 1942 or 1943, I lived through the great period of Hermeticism** during my studies with Longhi† at the University in Bologna, while I established naïve literary relationships with people my own age interested in these things; two of these were Francesco Leonetti and Roberto Roversi, but Gaetano Arcangeli and later Alfonso Gatto, though older than we, were also with us. I was

[2] If it had been published in the more specialized magazine *Nuovi Argomenti*, for which it was written, it would have been something different from what it became.

* A small town near Casarsa.

** Hermeticism was the poetic movement contemporary with and countercultural to fascism; it emphasized difficult, sometimes symbolic language and imagery. Its main figures included two Nobel Prize winners: Eugenio Montale (1896–1981), and Salvatore Quasimodo (1901–68), and Giuseppe Ungaretti (1888–1970).

† Roberto Longhi (1890–1970): art critic and historian, editor of the cultural review *Paragone*; Pasolini dedicated his second film, *Mamma Roma* (with Anna Magnani) to him; Leonetti (b. 1924), a playwright and poet, plays Herod II in *The Gospel According to Saint Matthew*; Roversi (b. 1923) is a poet and critic; Arcangeli (1910–69) was

rather young to be a university student, though I lived through that period as both apprentice and initiate. In 1942, in fact, my first volume of poetry, *Poems of Casarsa*, was published, at my own expense, by the Libreria Antiquaria of Signor Landi. I was exactly twenty, but I had begun to write the poems collected in it three years earlier at Casarsa, my mother's village, where we went every year for our poor vacations with our relatives, since my father's small salary as an officer didn't allow us to go anywhere else.

They were poems in the Friulian dialect: the *hésitation prolongée entre le sens et le son*[3] had made an apparently definitive choice, in favor of sound; and the semantic dilation worked upon sound had gone so far as to transfer the semantemes into another linguistic domain, from whence they would return as gloriously indecipherable.

Two weeks after the publication of the book, I received a postcard from Gianfranco Contini, saying he liked my book so much that he would review it immediately.

Who could ever describe my joy? I jumped and danced along the arcades of Bologna; as far as worldly satisfaction goes that one can aspire to when writing poems, what I felt that day in Bologna was so complete that I can absolutely and forever do without more of it. Contini's review didn't appear in *Primato* as he had planned, but abroad, in the *Corriere di Lugano* in Switzerland, a land, by definition, of exiles. And why? Because fascism, to my great surprise, did not concede the idea that the local particularisms and dialects of idle, stubborn people could exist in Italy. And so . . . my "pure language for poetry" had been mistaken for a realistic document proving the existence of poor eccentric peasants, or at least of peasants ignorant of the idealistic requirements of the Center . . . It's true that I'd stopped being a "natural" fascist that day in 1937 when I heard the poem by Rimbaud; but my anti-fascism now ceased to be purely cultural, because now I was experiencing the evil at first hand.

That was the winter we took refuge in Casarsa, and 1943 stands out as one of the most beautiful years of my life: "mi joventud, veinte años en tierre de Castilla!"[4]

I continued writing Friulian poems, but at the same time I began to write in Italian on similar themes. The Friulian of my poems had become exactly like the one spoken at Casarsa (and not a Friulian invented with the help of the Pirona Friulian-Italian dictionary) while my Italian, having been molded by dialect, acquired an ingenuous Romance-language freshness. Literary Italian—the new Latin, as it was called in those years, which was indebted to the Hermeticists, and above all to Leopardi—continued nevertheless to impose on me its inescapable elective and selective tradition; so I was writing verses ("Diaries") and keeping a journal, which continued following a central thread irrepressibly begun long before (and destined never to be extinguished), before the above-mentioned Friulian poems published in 1942. The latter then were, by comparison with my ambitiously literary productions, almost "*nugae*," trifles. Except that in this specific case, I

a poet; and Gatto (1909–76) was a poet and journalist who played Andrew in *The Gospel* and the doctor in *Teorema*.

[3] Valéry as quoted by Jakobson.

[4] Machado [trans.: from the poem "Fields of Castile"].

don't know how but certainly somehow, I knew, though perhaps without admitting it to myself, it was these very *nugae* that most mattered.

The Friulian poems were to be published later, in 1954, by Sansoni; while the Italian *nugae* that I had begun to write at that time would become *L'Usignolo della Chiesa Cattolica* [The Nightingale of the Catholic Church] (Longanesi, 1958). Meanwhile, I'd been drafted into the army for a few days, from September 1 to September 8, 1943. I returned to Casarsa from Pisa in rags, one shoe different than the other, after disobeying my officers' order to surrender arms to the Germans (on a canal near Leghorn), after walking one hundred kilometers and a thousand times nearly ending up on trains bound for Germany. I again started to write poems in Friulian and Italian, the rural splendors of *La meglio gioventù* [The Finest Youth] and *The Nightingale*. Which did not prevent me, however, from scribbling LONG LIVE LIBERTY on the walls, ending up in solitary confinement for the first time in my life, and thus experiencing what men of order are like. After that, I spent my days in hiding, hunted—very terrified, because at that time I was haunted by a decidedly pathological fear of death—continually obsessed by the idea that I would be hanged on a hook: for this was how young people who resisted the draft or declared themselves anti-fascists were punished on the Adriatic coast. My brother—three years younger than I, and now of draft age— left for the mountains to become an armed Partisan: I took him to the station (he had a gun hidden in a book). He was leaving as a communist; later, taking my advice (my having lived three years longer in the fascist period must have meant something to him), he joined the Action Party and the Osoppo Division.* Later still, some communists connected with Tito's army, which at the time intended to annex part of Friuli, killed him. The war ended, and the most tragic part of my life began (I continued writing *La meglio gioventù* and *The Nightingale*): my brother's death and my mother's immense grief; my father's homecoming from his wartime prison: a sick veteran, poisoned by the defeat of the fascists within the nation and the defeat of the Italian language at home; a ferocious wreck, a tyrant with no remaining power, crazed by too much bad wine, more and more in love with my mother who had never loved him as much as he did her, and who was now completely intent on her own grief; add to all this the problem of my life and flesh. In the winter of 1949, my dear reader, particularly dear to me because you are new and making use of a simple inexpensive collection, I escaped to Rome with my mother, as in a novel.

The Friulian period was over; my volumes of poems would lie in a drawer for a long time and would be published in the years mentioned above; but in Rome I immediately began writing those diaries again, in far less eccentric verse, within a literary and post-Hermetic matrix—which, as I said, I'd never stopped writing, not even in Romance-language Friuli, among its vineyards and mulberry trees. Later on, I collected a group of them under the title *Rome 1950* (and I would continue till the *Spring Sonnet*, Scheiwiller, 1960). But, a few months after my arrival in Rome, while I continued my anti-Italian–language research in a baroque

* The Partito d'azione was an anti-fascist party formed in exile in Paris, with a philosophical base in "liberal socialism" and "liberal revolution"; Osoppo is a town in Friuli.

and Gaddian* key, which I had started in a Romance and native key in Friuli, I began to write that narrative later published as *Ragazzi di vita*** (1955).

In Rome, at first I lived at Piazza Costaguti, near the Portico d'Ottavia (the ghetto!), then I went to the ghetto of outlying slums, near the Rebibbia jail, in a house that remained forever without a roof (the rent was 13,000 lire a month). For two years I was desperately unemployed, one of those people who end up committing suicide; then I found a teaching job in a private school at Ciampino for 27,000 lire a month. In my Rebibbia house in the poor outlying slums, I began—through a slow transformation and fusion of my anti-Italian component, often in an artificial voice, a falsetto (which had produced the dialect verses, and other things) and with my diaries' classicist component—my truly real "poetic work"—from *The Ashes of Gramsci* to *Poetry in the Form of a Rose*.

As I've said so many times in the course of so many interviews that it's now become almost a mechanism to turn the conversation to my own interests (in order to bend reality to my designs): what made me a communist was the Friulian farm-workers' struggle against the owners of the large estates and farms immediately after the war. (*The Days of Lodo De Gasperi* was supposed to be the title of my first novel, later published as *Il sogno di una cosa* [The Dream of Something].) I sided with the workers. Later, I read Marx and Gramsci.

The transformation and fusion, which I referred to above, of my two poetic mainstreams, the anti-Italian, in falsetto, and the high-Italian, takes place under the sign of my never-orthodox Marxism. It was only slowly that I arrived at the "civil poem" on the ashes of Gramsci; the entire first part of the volume, from "L'Appenino" ["The Apennine"] to "L'umile Italia" ["Humble Italy"] is prehistoric with respect to it: in the Roman subproletarian slums, there still exists the pre-Alpine spirit of clean lands and newly planted cedars that accumulates formally, especially in the spaces made obligatory by the necessity of rhyme (of tercets), in the guise of delaying elements. I realize now, though, that very little has changed substantially within me or outside me from the times of the farm-laborers' struggle to the present. As I write this introduction for a nonspecialized reader, I'm working on a document about the strike of Roman streetcleaners ("Appunto per un romanzo sull'immondezza" ["Notes for a Novel about Garbage"]), and it doesn't really seem that nearly thirty years have gone by. It could be that the sentiments of class struggle of the young in 1968–70 have recalled those great days; and it's not important if this is an illusion. In fact, the class struggle is not a phenomenon that can be resolved in thirty years, and its characteristics are always the same.

Finally, the poems selected here from the volumes representing the thirteen years between 1951 and 1964 form a coherent and compact block. What strikes me in them—I'm talking as if I'd become estranged from them, which isn't true at all—is a widespread sense of discouraging unhappiness: an unhappiness that's part of the language itself, like a datum of its own, reducible in quantity and almost in physicality. This sense (almost a right) of being unhappy is so pre-

---

* Carlo Emilio Gadda (1893–1973), novelist who made extensive use of Roman dialect idioms in his writings.
** Published as *The Ragazzi* by Grove Press, New York, 1968.

dominant that the sensual joy (of which the book is full, though accompanied by the sense of guilt) is obscured by it; and so is its civil idealism. What strikes me further, on reading these poems, is the realization of how ingenuous was the expansiveness with which I wrote them: it was as if I were writing for someone who could only love me a great deal. I understand now why I have been the object of so much suspicion and hatred.

NOTES

THE ASHES OF GRAMSCI

Note by Pasolini: Gramsci is buried in a little grave in the English Cemetery, which is between Saint Paul's Gate and the Testaccio quarter, not far from Shelley's grave. Written on his stone is the simple inscription: "Cinera Gramsci"—followed by the dates.

Translators' note: The great figure of Antonio Gramsci dominates postwar Italian politics and culture. Gramsci was born in Sardinia, January 22, 1891. He attended the University of Turin, along with Angelo Tasca, Umberto Terracini, and Palmiro Togliatti, with whom he founded the New Order movement and then, in 1921, after a schism with the Socialists, the Italian Communist Party (PCI). Tasca became the leader of the party's right wing. Togliatti became the PCI's leader after Gramsci's arrest in 1926, spent the latter part of the fascist period in the Soviet Union, and was PCI secretary general from 1945 until his death in 1964. From 1926 until his death in 1937, Gramsci remained in prison or prison hospital. During the incarceration—under the nose of Mussolini, his political opposite—Gramsci wrote, year after year, in countless notebooks and letters on problems of history, culture, politics, philosophy. These writings, published in many volumes after the war, profoundly affected the debate on the course of postwar Italian life, as Italians brought the vocabulary and principles of Marxism into their discourse and as a vital Italian Communist Party increased in strength and influence throughout the 1960s and 1970s.

In English, Gramsci is represented by *The Modern Prince and Other Writings* (New York: International Publishers, 1959); *Prison Notebooks* (New York: International Publishers, 1971); *Letters from Prison* (New York: Harper, 1973), as well as by two volumes of his early writings: *Selections from Political Writings, 1910–1920* (New York: International Publishers, 1976) and *History, Philosophy and Culture in the Young Gramsci* (Saint Louis: Telos Press, 1975). There are many studies of Gramsci's thought, and several biographies, including one translated from Italian: Giuseppe Fiori, *Antonio Gramsci, Life of a Revolutionary* (London: New Left Books, 1970; New York: Schocken paperback, 1973).

p. 3: *Latium:* the region of Italy in which Rome is located.
p. 3: *that Italian May:* the beginning of World War I, May 24, 1915.

p. 5: *Testaccio:* a poor quarter of Rome on the east side of the Tiber, across the river from Trastevere.

p. 13: *Verano:* Rome's municipal cemetery, where a poor Roman would be buried.

p. 17: *Maremma:* a swampy area in Southern Tuscany, noted for its melancholy atmosphere. *Versilia:* the Northern Tuscan coastline between Massa and Viareggio, the Apuan Alps and the Tyrrhenian Sea.

p. 17: *Cinquale:* a small river in Versilia.

THE TEARS OF THE EXCAVATOR

p. 25: *Viale Marconi:* a road bordering *Trastevere* (which means "Trans-Tiber"), one of the old neighborhoods of Rome (located on the west side of the Tiber), which in the 1950s still was a working-class district, but is now increasingly inhabited by the wealthy, bourgeois, and artists. The poem's time and location shift between the present (1956), when Pasolini was living in Trastevere (parts I and III–VI) and the first years in Rome (1950–52), when he was living in a slum on the outskirts of the city near the Rebibbia jail (part II and the last half of III).

p. 31: *Fiumicino:* a coastal suburb of Rome.

p. 35: *Janiculum:* one of the hills of Rome, which dominates the city's landscape and on which are the Renaissance-era Villa Doria Pamphili, now open to the public, and the Piazzale Garibaldi, laid out as a boulevard, where Garibaldi made a stand for the Roman republic against papal troops in 1849. Trastevere sits below the Janiculum.

p. 39: *Gobetti,* Piero (1901–26): founded the biweekly *New Energies* in 1918. A liberal Turinese intellectual, he came very close, in his anti-fascism, to Marxism; his ideas grew from the belief that only the proletariat could defeat fascism. Despite police harassment, he continued publishing until 1925, when he was ordered by the government to stop. He chose exile in Paris, and died there of pneumonia. *Croce,* Benedetto (1866–1952): neo-Hegelian critic, historian, philosopher, and the dominant figure in Italian intellectual life in the first half of this century. A non-Marxist and anti-fascist, he wrote over forty volumes on aesthetics, ethics, economics, history, historiography, and poetry, including books on Shakespeare and Dante.

THE RELIGION OF MY TIME

p. 57: *Bologna, Casarsa:* the latter is a small town in the Friuli region of Italy; Pasolini spent much of his first twenty years in these two places.

p. 63: *Tommaseo,* Niccolò (1802–72), romantic, polemical poet. *Carducci,* Giosue (1835–1907), the major Italian poet of the second half of the nineteenth century. Though fiercely anticlerical, his poetry expressed a lofty religious sense of life. He taught literature from 1860 to 1904 at the University of Bologna, where Pasolini later studied. He was awarded the 1906 Nobel Prize for literature.

p. 65: *The Songs of the Greek People,* a collection of Greek songs compiled by Tommaseo.

p. 67: *Tagliamento*: a river about a mile outside Casarsa.

p. 71: *Donna Olimpia*: a street in the Monteverde section of Rome on the Janiculum. *Villa Sciarra*: a park on the Janiculum above Trastevere.

p. 83: *Note by Pasolini*: This person, in whose company I was going along "the dark tunnel of the boulevards,/at the edge of the city, cruised by lost/souls, uncrowned dirty crucifixes," etc., until arriving at the sea at Tor Vajanica, is none other than Federico Fellini.

p. 85: *Tor Vajanica*: a suburb of Rome on the sea.

p. 89: *Piazza del Popolo*: one of Rome's main squares, below the Pincio Park and Villa Borghese.

p. 97: *Nightingale of the Catholic Church*: A 1958 collection of poems Pasolini wrote in Casarsa from 1943 to 1949—when the influence of his natal Catholicism was giving way to that of Marxism—bears this title.

p. 103: *in that poor meadow*: in Casarsa, where his younger brother Guido, a Catholic partisan killed by some Communist partisans in a power struggle in February 1945, is buried. Pier Paolo is now buried close by.

REALITY

p. 111: *Canossa*: a hamlet in the Emilia region, where there is a ruined castle on a hill, scene of the penance of Henry IV of the Holy Roman Empire before Pope Gregory VII in 1077.

p. 121: *Salvatore Giuliano*: a Sicilian bandit, active 1945–48. He became something of a folk hero, almost like a Robin Hood, and for a time was courted by political forces in Sicily. He was finally caught and killed in a police ambush in 1948.

A DESPERATE VITALITY

p. 149: *Fiumicino*: the coastal suburb of Rome where Leonardo da Vinci airport is located. *Godard*: Pasolini refers to Jean-Luc Godard's film *Contempt*, made in 1963 on location in Rome, with Michel Piccoli (as the "French screenwriter"), Brigitte Bardot, Fritz Lang (playing himself) and Jack Palance. *Moravia*, Alberto (b. 1907): leading Italian novelist; from 1966 coeditor with Pasolini of *Nuovi Argomenti*, Italy's most prestigious literary journal; close friend of Pasolini's; for many years husband of Elsa Morante. *Contempt* is based on his early novel *Il disprezzo*, published in English as *Ghost at Noon*.

pp. 163, 165: *Appian Ways, Centocelles, Tuscolanas, Capanellas, Casilinas*: all used here to refer to working-class and subproletarian quarters of Rome. *Caetanis, Torlonias*: ancient wealthy Roman landowning families.

PLAN OF FUTURE WORKS

p. 183: *Piero* della Francesca (1420–92): the great Umbrian painter notable for the luminous clarity and precision of his frescoes. *Sicilian*: in the thirteenth century, Sicily was the literary center of Italy. *appendixes* (such places as Italy) *of the exquisite Centers* (the United States and the Soviet Union). *Frederick* the Great: from 1215 to 1250 the emperor of the Holy Roman Empire, which included Germany and had Sicily as its southern tip.

p. 185: *"Blasphemy"* or *"The Divine Mimesis"*: The first is a poem by Pasolini; the second is a long prose work begun in 1963. Dantesque in scope as well as title, it is, according to its "editor" (Pasolini), the notes of a poet found killed "with the blows of a club" near Palermo. It was published in fragments only in 1974, a year before Pasolini's own murder "with the blows of a club" near Rome.

p. 187: *lettera 22*: a cheap Olivetti portable typewriter.

p. 189: *the Bel Paese where the* No *sounds:* cf. Dante, *Inferno,* xxx, 80: *del bel paese là dove 'l sì suona.*

p. 193: *mi joventud:* from Antonio Machado (1875–1939) *Canciones,* "Fields of Castile": "My youth, twenty years on the soil of Castile!"

p. 195: *Bellonci,* Maria (b. 1902): writer of popular biographies of Lucrezia Borgia and the Gonzagas. It is at her home in Rome that the Strega literary prize is voted on each year. *Quirinale:* Italy's presidential palace on the Quirinal hill in Rome. *Corriere della Sera:* based in Milan, one of Italy's two or three major newspapers, which at the time of the poem's composition, the early 1960s, had a conservative orientation. By 1970, when the paper, with Italy, had moved leftward, Pasolini was regularly writing often controversial columns for it, as frequently as three times a week, many of which were given prominent display on the front page. Some of these have been issued as *Scritti corsari,* with a preface by Alberto Moravia (Milan: Garzanti, 1975).

p. 195: *Soldati,* Mario (b. 1906): born in Turin. Novelist, journalist, and film director. *Piovene,* Guido (b. 1907): born in Vicenza. Novelist and journalist. *Landolfi,* Tommaso (1908–1979): born in Pico. Short-story writer and novelist, translator of Russian and German literature. Two collections of his stories are available in English, *Gogol's Wife* and *Cancerqueen.*

ONE OF THE MANY EPILOGS

p. 207: Pasolini discovered the teenage Ninetto Davoli while he was preparing the *Gospel.* Ninetto, who was from Calabria via the Roman slums, was a natural comic actor. He played in most of Pasolini's films from the *Gospel* on, starring with the Neapolitan comic Totò in *Hawks and Sparrows* and playing central roles in the *Trilogy of Life* films of the 1970s. It was a complex relationship—sexual, artistic, familial—and Ninetto was surely Pasolini's great mature love. Ninetto's 1972 marriage strained the relationship, but the two remained close up to the poet's death. At the time of the poem's composition, September 1969, Ninetto was serving in the army, and Pasolini visited him at the Arezzo base, where Ninetto was in punitive custody for having been absent without leave.

TRANSLATORS'
NOTE

We have translated about a sixth of Pasolini's published Italian poems and none at all of his Friulian lyrics. Our choices from *Le ceneri di Gramsci* (1957), *La religione del mio tempo* (1961), and *Poesia in forma di rosa* (1964), were aided by the poet's own, made in 1970 for an inexpensive selection of his work. We have translated about 40 percent of that book. We consulted the 1973 French selection from Gallimard in a translation by José Guidi overseen by Pasolini. We also include poems from *Trasumanar e organizzar* (1971). The dates of composition (at the end of each poem) for the following poems are probable estimates: "Supplica a mia madre," "La realtà," "Le belle bandiere," "Una disperata vitalità," "L'Alba meridionale," "Versi del Testamento," and "La poesia della tradizione." The other poems were published with the dates as given.

We wish to thank Thelma Evelyn MacAfee, William Weaver, Jonathan Galassi, John Calder, Roger Evans, Alice and William Randall, the PEN American Center for giving Norman MacAfee its 1979 Renato Poggioli award and the Columbia University Translation Center for a 1978 award, Eleanor Murdock, Timothy Cleary, Graziella Chiarcossi, Giuseppe Zigaina, Enzo Siciliano, John Shepley, Piera Oppezza, Maria Farber; the New York Italian Cultural Institute's Marco Miele, Maddalena Raimondi, and Ana Maria Gargotta; Miriam Hood, Edward Orff, and Robert Foy, of the New York Public Library; Paul Willemen, Peter Broughan, and the British Film Institute; Vyt Bakaitas and the Anthology Film Archives, Louis Camp, Arthur Leone, Nancy Elliott, William Leo Coakley and Robin Prising, Fidel Zavala, Mark Braunstein, Stephen Hoffman, Jamie Schoen, Lawrence Venuti, Steven Wren, William Kelly, Kazuo Nakajima, Lynn Holst, Lothian Lynas of the New York Botanical Garden Library, Dallas Galvin, Inez Delgado de Torres, Michael Denneny, Charles Ortleb, Michael Andre, Dale Demy, Ana Pacheco.

ABOUT THE AUTHOR

PIER PAOLO PASOLINI was born in Bologna on
March 5, 1922 and graduated from its university.
In 1949 he moved to Rome, and there found work
in the burgeoning Italian film industry, while
writing the poems and novels that were to make
his reputation as the most outspoken and gifted
writer of his generation. His novels about Roman
underclass youth created scandals when they were
published in the late fifties; his groundbreaking
book of poems, *The Ashes of Gramsci*, appeared
in 1957, to be followed by *The Religion of My
Time* (1961), *Poetry in the Form of a Rose* (1964),
To Transfigure, To Organize (1971) and more
than forty other volumes of poetry, fiction, and
cultural and social criticism.

Pasolini's first feature film, *Accattone*, appeared
in 1961, to be followed by *Mamma Roma, The
Gospel According to Saint Matthew* (which made
him internationally famous), *Hawks and Sparrows,
Oedipus Rex, Teorema, Medea, The Decameron,
Canterbury Tales, The Arabian Nights* and the
scandalous *Salò: The 120 Days of Sodom*, to name
only the best-known. In his later years, Pasolini
published a great deal of political and cultural
criticism, much of it written for *Corriere della
Sera*, Milan's daily newspaper. He was murdered
on November 2, 1975.

THE TRANSLATOR

NORMAN MACAFEE, poet, editor and translator, was
born in Philadelphia and is a graduate of the
universities of Pennsylvania and Iowa. His
translations of Pasolini's poems won the 1979
Renato Poggioli Award of the P.E.N. American
Center. He lives in New York. His collaborator,
LUCIANO MARTINENGO, is an Italian film maker and
writer living in Milan.